The VINEGAR Book

by Emily Thacker

Table of Contents

Chapter One

Stay Young Forever

So you want to live forever!

Apple cider vinegar contains the healthy goodness of apples, concentrated into a teaspoon of golden liquid. It is packed with essential amino acids and healthful enzymes. And so it comes as no surprise that some individuals have claimed this natural storehouse of vitamins and minerals will cure all that ails mankind — and even extend life and youthfulness.

Is apple cider vinegar an instant remedy for all the ills of this world? A magical nostrum? A mystical elixir? A liquid cure all? Some believe it is something very close to this!

Traditional medical systems are sickness oriented — designed to respond to illness. But good health, and extending the prime of life, begins with a body which is maintained, every single day, by good eating and health practices. A healthy, ageless body requires a diet rich in a wide assortment of nutrients. And the safest way to get adequate nutrients is to supply the body with a varied diet. It should meet all known nutritional requirements and be enhanced with lots of trace elements.

Perhaps this is why apple cider vinegar has the reputation of being an almost magical tonic — one of the most healthful, nutrient filled fluids known to mankind. A teaspoon of this golden liquid supplies a generous portion of the building blocks needed to be a healthy person. This potent substance is endowed with a multitude of vitamins, minerals and essential amino acids.

Scientists know humans need very tiny amounts of hundreds of as yet largely unidentified compounds. Nutritional researchers are constantly discovering minerals, enzymes, amino acids, and other substances and essences the body needs for complete health. Exactly how the body uses trace elements remains a medical mystery. Nor has science identified the amount needed of most of them.

Doctors do know a tiny deficiency, a missing milli-micro-gram of an important element can result in sickness, premature aging, or damage to the mind. The best advice nutritional scientists can give is to eat a diet of assorted foods, making a broad spectrum of nutrients available to the body.

Since the beginning of time mankind has sought the magic elixir which bubbles from the fabled "Fountain of Youth." For most of us, apple cider vinegar may be as close as we'll ever come to such a universal remedy. Because, you see, the secret to eternal youth is already ours. It is simply to be vital and able to enjoy a zestful, vigorous, life every single day we live.

So, it is no wonder apple cider vinegar is a time-honored prescription for those who want to retain vitality and good health well into old age. Through the ages it has been prescribed as an aid in maintaining general health, preventing disease, controlling weight, easing the discomfort of coughs, colds and breathing difficulties, and settling a disturbed digestive system.

Because old-time remedies (such as those in this book) are handed down from parent to child to grandchild, over many generations, changes occur. Families develop their own variations. Yet, there is one constant theme: some small amount of apple cider vinegar, taken each day, somehow brings better health and longer life. Some of these old-time beliefs about what apple cider vinegar could do follow (remember, these are only folk remedies, not scientifically proven cures!):

LIVE A LONG, HEALTHY, VITAL LIFE

Ensure long life and health by drinking vinegar every day. Simply add a tablespoon to a full glass of water and drink it down.

The way to stay healthy and alert, well into old age, is to combine 1 teaspoon of vinegar, 1 teaspoon of honey, and a full glass of water. Take this tonic 3 times a day, 1/2 hour before meals.

For a long, vigorous life, filled with robust good health, sip a vinegar tonic, very slowly, before each meal. Mix together and begin drinking immediately: 1 cup warm water, 2 tablespoons apple cider vinegar, and 1 teaspoon honey.

The most palatable way to take a daily dose of vinegar is to add a small dollop of clover honey to a tablespoon of vinegar and a teaspoon of olive oil. Mix it all together and drip this healthy dressing over a small bowl of greens.

A health promoting salad dressing can be made from 1/4 cup vinegar, 1/4 cup corn oil, and 1/8 cup honey. Mix well and serve at the evening meal to keep the whole family in good health.

Memory can be greatly improved by drinking a glass of warm water before each meal, with a teaspoon of apple cider vinegar stirred in.

FIGHT GERMS

To relieve the pain of a sore throat caused by a cold, mix together 1/4 cup honey and 1/4 cup apple cider vinegar. Take 1 tablespoon every 4 hours. May be taken more often if needed.

Ease the discomfort of a sore throat and speed healing by sipping occasionally on a syrup made of 1/2 cup apple cider vinegar, 1/2 cup water, 1 teaspoon cayenne pepper, and 3 tablespoons honey.

A vinegar gargle can ease the pain of a sore throat. Just gargle with a glass of warm water to which a tablespoon of apple cider vinegar has been added. Repeat as needed. This also acts as a great mouthwash!

Soothe a dry night cough by sprinkling the pillowcase with apple cider vinegar.

A small amount of vinegar, taken every day, keeps the urinary tract nice and acidy. This is useful to reduce the likelihood of getting a kidney or bladder infection.

To chase away a cold, soak an eight-inch square of brown paper (cut from a paper grocery bag) in apple cider vinegar. When the paper is saturated, sprinkle it with pepper and bind to the chest with cloth strips, pepper side of the paper next to the skin. After 20 minutes, remove the paper and wash the chest, being careful not to become chilled.

LOOK BETTER, FEEL BETTER

The most marvelous tonic for the feet is to walk back and forth in ankle deep bath water to which 1/2 cup apple cider vinegar has been added. Do this for 5 minutes, first thing in the morning, and for 5 minutes before retiring in the evening. Hot, aching feet will feel cooled and soothed.

If troubled by the itching and peeling of athlete's foot, soak socks or hose in vinegar water. Mix 1 part vinegar with 5 parts water and soak for 30 minutes before washing as usual.

A full head of healthy, richly colored hair can be ensured, well into old age. You need only to start each day with a glass of water to which has been added 4 teaspoons each of apple cider vinegar, black strap molasses, and honey.

Apple cider vinegar is helpful in melting away excess pounds. Simply drink a glass of warm water, with a single teaspoon of apple cider vinegar stirred in, before each meal. It moderates the over-robust appetite and melts away fat.

Now, whether vinegar actually burns up fatty calories, reins in the over-lusty inclination for partaking of provisions, or simply fills one up with tart vinegar-water, the results are the same. You eat less and the pounds melt away!

Asthma can be relieved by combining the advantages of accupressure with the benefits of apple cider vinegar. Use a wide rubber band to hold gauze pads, which have been soaked in vinegar, to the inside of the wrists.

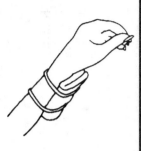

Heavily soiled hands can be cleaned, while giving them a soothing treatment. Simply scrub with cornmeal, moistened with apple cider vinegar. Then rinse in cool water and pat dry.

You can banish dandruff and make hair shiny and healthy if you rinse after every shampoo with: one-half cup apple cider vinegar mixed into two cups of warm water.

Use a vinegar and water rinse to eliminate frizz from over-permed hair. It also brightens dark hair and adds sparkle to blond hair.

Ensure soft, radiant skin and prevent blemishes by conditioning the skin while sleeping with a covering of strawberries and vinegar. Mash 3 large strawberries into 1/4 cup vinegar and let it sit for 2 hours. Then strain the vinegar through a cloth. Pat the strawberry flavored vinegar onto the face and neck. Wash off in the morning. Skin will soon be free of pimples and blackheads.

Corns and calluses will fall away, overnight, if you treat them with a vinegar compress. Simply tape 1/2 of a slice of stale bread (which has been soaked with apple cider vinegar) to the offending lump. By morning the skin will look smooth and new.

Ladies can protect their skin from the ravages of the summer sun by applying a protective of olive oil and apple cider vinegar. Mixed half and half, this combination helps prevent sunburn and chapping.

Age spots (some call them liver spots) can be gotten rid of if you wipe them daily with onion juice and vinegar. 1 teaspoon onion juice and 2 teaspoons vinegar should be mixed together and applied with a soft cloth. Or, 1/2 a fresh onion can be dipped into a small dish of vinegar and then rubbed across the offending skin. In a few weeks the spot will begin to fade.

Itchy welts and hives, swellings, and blemishes can be eased by the application of a paste made from vinegar and cornstarch. Just pat it on and feel the itch being drawn out as the paste dries.

Relieve the discomfort and unsightliness of varicose veins by wrapping the legs with a cloth wrung out of apple cider vinegar. Leave this on, with the legs propped up, for 30 minutes, morning and evening. Considerable relief will be noticed within 6 weeks. To speed up the healing process, follow each treatment with a glass of warm water, to which a teaspoon of apple cider vinegar has been added. Sip slowly, and add a teaspoon of honey if feeling overtired.

EASE PAIN & SUFFERING

Headaches will fade away if you follow this simple procedure: add a dash of apple cider vinegar to the water in a vaporizer and inhale the vapors for 5 minutes. Lay quietly and the headache should be relieved in 20 minutes.

Hiccups will disappear if you sip, very slowly, a glass of warm water with 1 teaspoon of vinegar in it. This works even better if you sip from the far side of the glass!

An unsettled stomach will calm down if you sip quietly on a glass of very warm water, to which has been added 1 tablespoon honey and 1 tablespoon vinegar. This is also good for easing gas.

If a headache will not go away, try a paper bag hat. Soak the bottom of the open edges of a brown paper bag in apple cider vinegar. Put the bag on the head (like a chef's hat) and tie it in place with a long scarf. The headache should be relieved in 45 minutes.

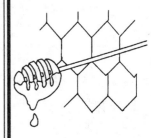

Those plagued with nighttime leg cramps can find relief by supplementing meals with a glass of water, fortified with apple cider vinegar.

Prevent leg cramps by combining 1 teaspoon honey, 1 teaspoon apple cider vinegar, and 1 tablespoon calcium lactate in 1/2 glass of water. This is taken once a day.

Soothe tired or sprained muscles by wrapping the afflicted area with a cloth wrung out of apple cider vinegar. Leave it on for 3 to 5 minutes and repeat as needed. For extra special relief, add a good dash of cayenne pepper to the vinegar.

Banish the discomfort of nausea or vomiting by placing a cloth wrung out of warm apple cider vinegar on the stomach. Replace with another warm cloth when it cools.

Chapter Two

Vinegar Fights Disease*

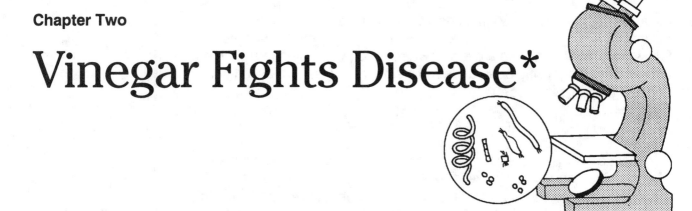

Apple cider vinegar enthusiasts can recite a long list of ailments it is reported to be able to cure or prevent. It is claimed vinegar can banish arthritis, forestall osteoporosis, prevent cancer, kill infection, condition the skin, aid digestion, control weight, preserve memory, and protect the mind from aging.

On the pages which follow, some of the most recent findings of medical researchers, and the way this research impacts on vinegar therapy, are recorded. Also included are some of the more enduring traditional remedies.

Tannins are naturally astringent preservatives

Cider is a blend of juices pressed from chopped apples

Can apple cider vinegar possibly do all that is claimed for it? One answer may be: "Yes, because it is such a marvelous combination of tart good taste and germ killing acids." Vinegar is fermented from sweet apple cider, and takes its honey-gold color from tannins which flow from ruptured cell walls of fresh, ripe apples. When these naturally occurring, colorless preservatives, come into contact with air they develop the rich, golden color we associate with cider. This is called enzymatic browning. It contributes to the distinctive flavor of cider, a flavor with more spunk than simple apple juice.

Vinegar is made when fresh, naturally sweet cider is fermented into an alcoholic beverage (hard cider). Then it is fermented once again. The result is vinegar.

Apple cider vinegar contains more than thirty important nutrients, a dozen minerals, over half a dozen vitamins and essential acids, and several enzymes. Plus, it has a large dose of pectin for a healthy heart.

When apple cider vinegar is exposed to heat and air, it gives off some hints of its character. Take a healthy sniff and what you inhale is the 'volatile' part of vinegar — the portion which will evaporate easily. Scientists

Please remember, if you have a specific illness, or take medication regularly, discuss the effects of adding vinegar to your diet with your doctor.

recently analyzed this small part of what vinegar is. They found 93 different volatile components they were able to recognize, plus others as yet to be classified! Vinegar has:

7 Hydrocarbons   7 Bases
18 Alcohols   3 Furans
4 Acids   13 Phenols
33 Carbonyls (4 aldehydes and 29 ketones)
8 Esters (plus 11 lactone esters)

The exact composition of a particular vinegar depends on what it was made from. Even apple cider vinegar varies with the kind and condition of the apples in it. Partly because of this, medical scientists do not always know exactly how or why it promotes healing. They do know it is both antiseptic and antibiotic.

VINEGAR'S EARLIEST MEDICAL USES

An early Assyrian medical text described the treatment for ear pain as being the application of vinegar.

In 400BC, Hippocrates (considered the Father of Medicine) used vinegar to treat his patients. This naturally occurring germ killer was one of the very first "medicines."

Vinegar was used as a healing dressing on wounds and infectious sores in Biblical times.

"Thieves Vinegar" got its name during the time of the Great Plague of Europe. Some enterprising thieves are said to have used vinegar to protect them from contamination while they robbed the homes of plague victims.

Vinegar is credited with saving the lives of thousands of soldiers during the U.S. Civil War. It was routinely used as a disinfectant on wounds.

VINEGAR AND THE SKIN

Historically, infections on the face, around the eyes, and in the ears have been treated with a solution of vinegar and water. It works because vinegar is antiseptic (it kills germs on contact) and antibiotic (it contains bacteria which is unfriendly to infectious microorganisms).

More recently, vinegar has been used to treat chronic middle ear diseases when traditional drug-based methods fail. One treatment

Vinegar has acetic acid, plus iso-butyric, lactic + propionic acids.

Cider contains phosphorus, potassium, chlorine, sodium, magnesium, sulfur, calcium, iron, flourine + silicon.

National Center for Health Statistics says ear infections are the most frequent diagnosis made by children's doctors.

currently being prescribed for ear infections at Ohio State University's hospital is irrigation with vinegar.

Doctors are currently considering the possibility of treating some eye infections with diluted vinegar. Right now, they are using it as a hospital disinfectant. One example of this use is at Yale-New Haven Hospital. When after-surgery eye infections became a problem, their Department of Bacteriology solved the problem with common vinegar. The hospital began routinely cleaning the scrub-room sink with a 1/2% solution of ordinary household vinegar. It worked better at eliminating the offending bacteria than the commercial product it replaced!

Two old-time remedies for treating mild burns were to douse the hurt with apple cider vinegar or to let a snail crawl over it. If you don't have a friendly snail around, you may want to try dabbing a bit of apple cider vinegar onto the painful area. Vinegar is particularly useful for neutralizing alkali burns.

Relieve itchy skin, too, by patting on apple cider vinegar. If the itch is near the eyes or other delicate areas dilute the vinegar, 4 parts water to 1 part vinegar. For a full body treatment, put 2 or 3 cups in the bath water. A handful of thyme can help, too.

Dampen a gauze square in apple cider vinegar and apply, gently, to ease rectal itching.

Use a cloth moistened in vinegar to clean armpits. Do not rinse it off and it will eliminate offensive odors for several hours.

Cool the burning of a sunburn by bathing in a tub of lukewarm water, to which a cup of apple cider vinegar has been added. Anytime a sprain or ache needs to be soaked in very hot water, a splash of vinegar in the water will make the water seem cooler.

One reason vinegar is so very helpful in treating skin disorders is that it has a pH which is nearly the same as healthy skin. So, applying vinegar helps to normalize the pH of the skin's surface.

VINEGAR, FIBER AND CHOLESTEROL

Vinegar contains a treasure trove of complex carbohydrates, as well as a good dose of that mysterious stuff called "dietary fiber." Both complex carbohydrates and dietary fiber have been recommended by the U.S. Surgeon General to help build resistance to cancer.

Ear infections heal faster if the ear is washed out with vinegar

About fibers ... yes, there are different kinds of fibers. Some are water soluble and some are not. A water soluble fiber soaks up water (adding bulk) but also has the power to interact with the body. Insoluble fibers soak up water (adding bulk) but do not interact with the body in the same complex way soluble fibers do.

When vinegar is made from fresh, natural apples it contains a healthy dose of pectin. Pectin is a soluble fiber. It dissolves in water, making it very available for the body to use. In addition to soaking up water, it slows down the absorption of food and liquid in the intestines. Therefore, it stays in the body longer than an insoluble fiber.

An insoluble fiber, such as wheat bran, rushes through the system. Particularly, it rushes through the intestines. This gives it laxative properties. Wheat bran may also produce large amounts of gas.

As pectin (apple cider vinegar fiber) works its slow, gentle way through the digestive system it binds to cholesterol. Then pectin pulls the cholesterol which is bound to it out of the body. Less cholesterol in the body makes for a reduced risk of cardiovascular problems, such as heart attacks and strokes.

VINEGAR AND DIGESTION

Apple cider vinegar is very similar to the chemicals found naturally in the stomach. Because of this, it has traditionally been hailed as an aid to digestion. And so, by improving digestion, it is felt it will improve the overall metabolism of the body.

Those who regularly imbibe of this elixir feel it helps cuts and abrasions heal faster, as well as speeding up the healing of more serious wounds.

Vinegar is considered by many to be able to attack and kill harmful bacteria which has invaded the digestive tract. This may lessen the likelihood of the body developing toxemia and other blood-borne infections.

Some doctors suggest regular vinegar use to prevent food poisoning. They recommend its use when visiting questionable restaurants or foreign countries. The usual dose is to take 1 tablespoon of vinegar, 30 minutes before meals. It can be mixed with a glass of water, vegetable juice, or any other beverage. Honey added to vinegar and water makes the taste more palatable for most people.

A vinegar experiment anyone can try is to use it to make legumes more digestible, and so less gas producing. Just splash a little vinegar in the pot when cooking dried beans. It will make them tender and easy on the digestive system.

Vinegar adds fiber + is low in fat, salt + sugar.

9

VINEGAR, BETA CAROTENE, AND CANCER

Aging, heart disease, cancer, and cataracts are symptoms of the harm done to the human body by free radicals, the "loose cannons" of the cell world. They damage chromosomes and are probably responsible for many of the physical changes associated with aging.

Free radicals roam through plants, animals, and humans, bouncing from cell to cell, damaging each in turn. Antioxidants absorb free radicals, making them harmless. Beta carotene, a carotenoid found in vinegar, is a powerful antioxidant.

Carotenoid occurs naturally in plants such as apples. Vinegar's beta carotene is in a natural, easy to digest form. One example of how this antioxidant contributes to maintaining good health is the way it protects the eye from cataracts. Cataract development is related to oxidation of the eye's lens. This happens when free radicals alter its structure. Studies show that eating lots of antioxidant containing foods decreases the risk of forming cataracts.

A correlation between eating lots of foods containing beta carotene and a lower risk of cancer has also been documented. Researchers, in more than 70 different studies, agree beta carotene lowers the risk of getting cancer. They include those at the State University of New York at Stony Brook, the University of Western Ontario in Canada, Tufts University, and Johns Hopkins School of Medicine.

In addition to giving cancer protection, beta carotene boosts the body's immune system. It works by attacking the free radicals which destroy the immune system.

Carotenoids are also the body's raw material for producing vitamin A, another potent antioxidant. They act together to protect from cancers associated with chemical toxins. According to National Cancer Research in England, when the body does not get enough vitamin A, it is particularly susceptible to cancers of the respiratory system, bladder and colon.

Old timers have long recommended taking a teaspoon of vinegar, every day, in a tall glass of vegetable juice. With all we now know about fiber and beta carotene, this may turn out to be very good advice!

VINEGAR AND MEMORY*

Memory loss is one of the most common and costly diseases of the elderly. Its price to this country is $44 billion a year, which is only the cost

Carotenoids probably protect plants from solar radiation.

A diet high in beta carotene helps prevent cataracts & cancer

10

in dollars. The real cost is in disrupted lives. Quality of life is ruined for those with memory loss, and often for their loved ones as well.

The three most common causes of memory loss are: Alzheimer's disease, multiple strokes (multi-infarct dementia) and alcohol abuse. Many other elders endure mental impairment caused by poor nutrition and reactions to prescription drugs.

Too often memory loss in individuals who are over 55 is treated as if it were irreversible or inevitable. Yet, information continues to pile up which proves memory loss can be successfully treated. More and more doctors are echoing the words of one specialist:

"...several of the causes are treatable, resulting in an arrest or actual reversal of the symptoms."

Diet is an important factor in control of risk factors for memory loss, and to reverse damage which has already been done. Good nutrition can decrease the likelihood of stroke by lowering cholesterol. It can also protect the mind from some of the worse causes of loss of mental function. The Journal of the American Dietetic Association puts it this way:

"Some forms of dementia — those due to excessive alcohol intake or vitamin deficiency — may be entirely preventable and partially reversible through diet."

Dementia which is associated with excessive alcohol intake is particularly treatable. The Journal goes on to say:

"In all types of dementia, adequate nutrition may improve physical well-being, help maximize the patients' functioning, and improve the quality of life."

Some studies indicate nutritional deficiencies are a problem for 36% of the over 80 year old population. And, nearly half of all nursing home patients have been shown to have some vitamin or mineral deficiency. These lower than normal levels of vitamins and minerals are important because they contribute to loss of mental ability. For example, memory loss is more frequent in patients who have lower than normal blood levels of vitamin B-12 and folate.

Apple cider vinegar supplies a balanced dose of vital amino acids, vitamins, and minerals that both the mind and body need for good health.

For more information about saving your memory, see the Order Form for Mind Power . . . Memory Magic!

The worst of the mind robbing diseases associated with aging is Alzheimer's disease (AD). Some studies show AD sufferers are particularly short of calcium, thiamin and niacin. And low serum B-12 levels have been reported in up to 30% of elderly patients with this kind of dementia. Almost every patient in a recent study of nutrient deficiencies showed complete recovery when given B-12 therapy. Folate supplements also proved valuable.

Thiamin deficiency is another nutritional cause of chronic memory problems. If the diet is sufficiently short of this nutrient, nerve cell loss and hemorrhages in the brain can result. Experts continue to remind us:

"...dietary modification may play an important role in the control of several ...diseases that may produce a dementia..."

The more we learn about good nutrition and the importance of getting an assortment of vitamins and minerals each day, the easier it is to understand old-time reliance on apple cider vinegar. One grandmother suggests this way to a healthy old age:

"Stir a teaspoon of apple cider vinegar and a teaspoon of honey into a glass of water and drink it with your meal. Do this 3 times a day to remain bright and alert all your life."

Treating malnutrition with megadoses of vitamins is being tested, with mixed results. Sometimes it is difficult to get the balanced dose a particular individual may need. And, there is always the possibility of doing harm by giving too many vitamins, or of giving an overdose of minerals. Vitamin therapy can also be expensive.

It is much better to prevent nutrient shortages by eating a balanced diet. And, for balancing the diet, it is hard to match the nutritional storehouse contained in a tablespoon of apple cider vinegar.

VINEGAR AND ARTHRITIS

Arthritis sufferers spend $8 to $10 billion each year searching for relief - relief that, too often, does not come. Those who are feeling the pain of arthritis will try almost anything to be free of the disease. This often results in large sums of money being spent on supposed cures which do not improve health, relieve chronic pain, or stop the progression of the disease.

The Select Committee on Aging's Subcommittee on Health and Long Term Care (House of Representatives, 98th Congress) calls the marketing of supposed arthritis cures a $10 billion a year scandal. In reporting on this, the Journal of the American Dietetic Association notes that both medical and nutrition authorities agree on one important fact about arthritis care:

The only specific treatment for arthritis is "weight control ... and a nutrient-dense diet ...."

This respected journal goes on to explain the conclusions nutritional scientists have drawn from studies of the eating habits of arthritis sufferers:

Sometimes the patient's diet is found to be "... grossly deficient in some nutrients."

Perhaps this helps to explain the long-standing belief by many that apple cider vinegar can play an important part in relieving the pain and slowing the progression of arthritis. At the very least it is less likely to hurt the one taking it than some of the more outrageous chemicals which have been advertised as being able to ease the symptoms of arthritis. And, in addition, it is inexpensive!

The time-honored vinegar recipe for dealing with arthritis is 1 teaspoon honey and 1 teaspoon apple cider vinegar, mixed into a glass of water and taken morning and evening.

Others believe the proper dose is to drink a glass of water, with 2 teaspoons vinegar in it, before each meal (3 times a day).

Another tonic which has often been recommended for those who suffer from arthritis' discomfort combines vinegar with celery, Epsom salts, and citrus (for vitamin C). Combine in a saucepan:

1/2 grapefruit	2 stalks celery
1 orange	4 cups water
1 lemon	

Cut the celery and fruit (including the peelings) into chunks. Simmer in water, uncovered, for 1 hour. Press the softened foods through a jelly bag and then stir in 1 tablespoon vinegar and 1 tablespoon Epsom salts. Drink a full glass of water, morning and evening, to which 1/4 cup of this tonic has been added.

With any of these vinegar regimens, expect it to take about a month for relief to begin. For more immediate results, many doctors say a gentle rubdown may help. One old-time liniment combines vinegar and oil with egg whites:

Epsom salts, which contain magnesium sulfate, have long been used to fight inflammation

Magnesium sulfate is called "Epsom salts" because it was once obtained by boiling down water from the English town of Epsom.

2 egg whites	1/2 cup vinegar
1/2 cup turpentine	1/4 cup olive oil

Mix all the ingredients together and use right away. Gently massage aching joints with this mixture, then wipe it off with a soft cloth. (Most all medical authorities would recommend leaving the turpentine out of this remedy, as it can cause skin irritation.)

VINEGAR AND IRON

Children, adolescents and adult women of child-bearing age should be sure to consume generous amounts of foods that are high in iron. The U.S. Surgeon General stresses that iron deficiency is a special problem for those in low-income families.

Others who should be sure they are getting lots of iron in their diets are high users of aspirin. Aspirin frequently causes intestinal blood loss, making the person at risk for iron deficiency.

One long-standing solution to low iron intake is to cook in iron pots. Each time one of these pans is used, some iron leaches into food. The higher the acid content of foods, the more iron will be absorbed into food. Adding a splash of vinegar to meats, sauces, and stews will raise their acid content. This increases the amount of iron they leach from iron pans.

To prevent anemia, the body needs iron, B-12, folate and a wide range of other nutrients. Apple cider vinegar delivers many of these nutrients, in an easy to digest and absorb form.

VINEGAR AND CALCIUM

Calcium is the most abundant mineral in the human body. Besides its well-known part in forming bones, calcium is necessary for many other parts of the body to work properly. Although only 1% of the body's calcium is found outside the skeleton, without this small amount muscles do not contract properly, blood clotting is affected, and neural function is seriously impaired.

Calcium absorption is affected by the amount of certain other substances in the body. For example, a diet too rich in phosphorus can cause calcium not to be absorbed properly. Or, eating too much protein can interfere with calcium absorption. Then, even if enough calcium is eaten, the body cannot draw it out of food and use it.

15 to 20 million Americans currently suffer from osteoporosis

Osteoporosis is literally porous bones!

Each year over 300,000 women suffer fractured hips. 200,000 will never return to normal life. Nearly 45,000 will die within six months of the fractures from complications. Other thousands find their spinal column begins to collapse, reducing height and producing the back deformity known as a widow's hump. Osteoporosis is a major factor in these disabling fractures.

As the body ages it is less and less efficient at pulling calcium from food. Complicating this is the fact that with age, people tend to take in less and less calcium. Some of this is because many older individuals develop lactose intolerance, causing them to drop calcium-rich dairy products from their diets.

And so it comes as no surprise that many individuals find their bones begin to shrink as they get older. As osteoporosis advances, bones decrease in both size and density. The result is porous, fragile bones that fracture easily. It is a serious health problem, causing deformity, disability, and pain.

Bones, you see, are living tissue. They are constantly being rebuilt and replaced. Whenever there is a shortage of calcium in muscles, blood, or nerves, the body pulls it from bones.

Apple cider vinegar contains a trace of needed calcium. It can also be used to dissolve calcium in soup bones. Several recent scientific reports show that when vinegar is added to the water in which soup bones are cooked, it leaches calcium from the bones and deposits it in the soup stock!

Some time-honored ways to combine vinegar and calcium, and some new ways medical research validates vinegar's use follow.

To make a delicious, low calorie, calcium-rich chicken soup you will need:

1/2	cup vinegar	2	bouillon cubes
3 lbs.	chicken bones	2	slightly beaten egg whites
3/4	cup tiny pasta	2	tablespoons chopped parsley

Begin with a gallon of water and at least 1/2 cup vinegar. Gently simmer 2 or 3 pounds of bones (chicken wings are a good choice) for about 2 hours, uncovered. Strain the broth and skim off all fat. Strip the meat from the bones and add the chicken, pasta, and bouillon cubes to the stock. Bring to a boil and cook for 10 minutes. Remove from heat and immediately dribble the egg whites into the hot liquid, stirring continuously. Mix in the parsley and serve. This soup is low calorie, healthy, and it adds calcium to the diet!

Cramps, gas and diarrhea after eating milk products are symptoms of lactose intolerance.

The inability to digest lactose, a sugar in dairy products, increases with age.

Research indicates cooking longer than 2 hours doesn't add much extra calcium.

The average adult diet includes only about 50% of the recommended level of calcium.

As little as one tablespoon of vinegar per quart of water can make a difference in the calcium which is pulled from boiled soup bones. A stronger vinegar solution (such as that used above) results in even more calcium being added to soup!

Another way to add calcium to the diet is to crumble feta cheese over torn greens. Use spinach, collards, beet tops, and kale, in addition to lettuce leaves. Sprinkle on a mixture of 2 tablespoons apple cider vinegar, 2 tablespoons honey, and 2 tablespoons water.

Newest research describes calcium supplements as being useful in the prevention and treatment of osteoporosis. And so, many doctors and nutritionists recommend them. Calcium supplements are prescribed for those with calcium deficient diets, elders who do not metabolize calcium adequately, and for those with increased calcium needs (this can include postmenopausal women). This calcium is usually added to the diet by taking calcium tablets, or in the form of antacid tablets.

The US Pharmacopeia Convention sets standards for drugs. It says a calcium tablet should dissolve in a maximum time of 30 minutes. An antacid tablet should be completely broken down in 10 minutes. If a tablet takes longer to break up than the recommended time, its usefulness is seriously impaired.

Studies estimate that more than half of the popular calcium supplements on the market do not meet the recommended timetable. Yet, calcium supplements can only be properly used by the body if they disintegrate in a reasonable length of time after being taken.

A simple to use vinegar test can tell you whether or not your calcium supplement dissolves in time for your body to digest it properly:

• Drop the calcium supplement tablet into three ounces of room temperature vinegar.

• Stir briskly, once every five minutes.

• At the end of 30 minutes the tablet should be completely disintegrated.

Tests by medical researchers found that times varied widely among the most popular brands. One brand of calcium supplement tablet broke up, completely, in three minutes. Another popular brand tablet was still mostly intact after 30 minutes.

15 to 20 million Americans are affected by osteoporosis. This contributes to the 1.3 million bone fractures, every year, that occur in

individuals over 45 years old. Over the years, this adds up to a lot of disability. For example, one out of every three women over 65 has at least one fractured vertebra. When these tiny back bones crack, they can cause disabling pain.

Hip fractures are an even bigger problem. By 90 years of age, one out of every six men and one out of every three women will have suffered a fractured hip. One out of each five hip fractures leads to death. Long term nursing care is required for many others. All told, osteoporosis costs this country more than $10 billion every year.

As the body ages, the stomach produces less acid. Some believe this fact contributes to calcium shortages in elders. After all, acid is needed to dissolve almost all calcium supplement tablets. One solution may be to take calcium supplements with an old-fashioned vinegar tonic. It not only has acid for dissolving calcium, it adds the bit of extra calcium which is in vinegar!

VINEGAR AND BORON

Have you had your boron today? If you began the day with apple cider vinegar your body is probably well fortified against boron deficiency. This critical trace element is needed for good health and strong bones.

Boron is a mineral which is necessary for both plant and animal life. When it is not readily available to plants, they do not grow properly. Some become dwarfs and others crack and become disfigured. The human body does not make strong, straight bones when it is missing from the diet. One reason for this is that boron plays a critical role in the way the body uses calcium. Without boron, calcium cannot form and maintain strong bones.

When vinegar releases its boron into the body, all sorts of wonderfully healthy things begin to happen. Boron affects the way steroid hormones are released. Then it regulates both their use and how long they stay active in the body.

How boron builds bones is just now beginning to be understood by scientists. One of the few things they do know is it makes changes in the way the membrane around individual cells works.

The boron and hormone connection is vital to bone formation. Blood and tissue levels of several steroid hormones (such as estrogen and testosterone) increase dramatically in the presence of boron. Both of these are needed to complete the calcium-to-bone growth cycle. This

Beware: bone meal is sometimes recommended as a calcium supplement, may contain toxic amounts of lead!

17

relationship between hormones, boron, and calcium helps to explain why estrogen replacement is about the only treatment for osteoporosis.

Some other trace elements necessary for maintaining bone mass are manganese, silicon, and magnesium. Some doctors recommend supplements of all of them for post-menopausal women, even though no one knows exactly how they work. Many feel boron is useful for treating a lot of the ailments (such as arthritis) that doctors are not able to treat successfully with drugs.

We do know that apple cider vinegar supplies boron, as well as manganese, silicon, and magnesium to the body. Even more important, it does so in a balanced-by-nature way.

JAPANESE RICE VINEGAR AND HEALTH

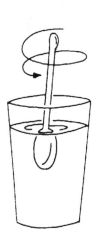

Taking vinegar and honey as a life enhancing tonic is more than merely an American custom. In Japan it is an old favorite, too.

Japan's most famous vinegar is made from rice. The bulk of Japanese commercial vinegar is made from wine leftovers. The sediment left from the production of the rice wine called "sake" is used to make industrial vinegar. These dregs, called "lees," produce a vinegar which is similar in nutrient value to our white vinegar.

The rice vinegar which is used for cooking and healing remedies is made directly from brown rice. Belief in the healing nature of this deeply colored rice vinegar has come down through thousands of years of Japanese culture.

Some ways of using vinegar that have endured for centuries - and some of Japan's newest research into the healing power of rice vinegar follow:

According to the Japan Food Research Laboratories, vinegar made directly from brown rice has five times the amount of amino acids as the commercial product made from lees. Perhaps the healthful benefits of rice vinegar are because of the 20 amino acids it contains. Or maybe it is the 16 organic acids which can be found in it.

The bottom of the bottle of even the best rice vinegar will have a fine rice sediment. When these grounds are disturbed they give the vinegar a muddy appearance. This dark residue is considered to be the mark of a high quality rice vinegar.

Recent research by Dr. Yoshio Takino, of Shizuka University in Japan, proved vinegar helps to maintain good health and slow down aging by helping to prevent the formation of two fatty peroxides. This is important to good health and long life in two important ways. One is associated with damaging free radicals. The other with the cholesterol formations which build up on blood vessel walls.

In Japan, vinegar is used to produce one of that country's most potent folk remedies. Tamago-su, or egg vinegar, is made by immersing a whole, raw egg in a cup of rice vinegar. The egg and vinegar are allowed to set, undisturbed, for seven days. During this time the vinegar dissolves the egg, shell and all.

At the end of one week the only part of the egg which has not been dissolved is the transparent membrane, located just inside the shell. The Tamago-su maker splits open this membrane and dumps its contents into the glass of vinegar. This piece of the egg is discarded and what remains is thoroughly mixed.

A small amount of this very powerful egg vinegar is taken three times a day, stirred into a glass of hot water. It is believed it will assure a long, healthy life. Traditionally, Samurai warriors considered egg vinegar tonic to be an important source of strength and power.

Vinegar is used as a bleaching agent on white vegetables. It also prevents enzymatic browning. When foods do not darken in air, they do not develop the off-taste associated with browning. Rice vinegar is also used in salad dressings, marinades, sauces, dips, and spreads.

Rice vinegar (like all vinegars) is a powerful antiseptic. It kills, on contact, dangerous bacteria such as salmonella and streptococcus.

The sushi industry is largely dependent on vinegar's ability to prevent germs from growing on the raw fish. It is sprinkled on the fish, included in dipping sauces, and used as a preservative.

Vinegar acts as a tenderizer on meats and vegetables used in stir-fry dishes.

Japanese housewives add a little rice vinegar to summer rice to prevent it from spoiling.

Vinegar, added to fish dishes, helps to eliminate the traditional fishy odor. It also helps get rid of fish smells at clean up time.

Enzymatic browning gives apple cider its color + tang.

Without vinegar, there would be no sushi!

Chapter Three

Where Did Vinegar Come From?

3,000 years before barley is grown to make beer—

4,000 years before all of Mesopotamia is engulfed in a disastrous flood—

5,000 years before wheeled vehicles appear in Sumeria or the Egyptians learn to plow—

—An enterprising householder prepares some fresh, naturally sweetened juice and seals it tightly in a stone jar. In a short time it ferments into the mildly intoxicating brew we call wine.

A very special day soon follows. The wine is left open to the air. A second fermentation takes place. Vinegar is created!

Imagine the surprise of the poor soul who took the first sip of this new brew. All the alcohol in the wine had turned into a sharp tasting acid! Had a partially filled wine cask been unknowingly set aside and left uncared for? Had a servant carelessly left the wine uncorked? Or could it possibly be ... did someone suspect the possibilities?

I've got the feeling vinegar has been around as long as apples!

No one knows for sure how it chanced to happen, but vinegar entered the world. And the event was momentous! Vinegar was found to be an almost universal preservative and cure-all. Vegetables submerged in this wonderful liquid kept their fresh color and crispness. Fish remained edible long after they should have rotted. Festering sores, when doused with it, began to heal. It only followed that mankind would confer an exalted status to this amazing concoction.

Our word "vinegar" comes from the French "vinaigre" - "VIN" for wine and "AIGRE" for sour. And that is just what it is: wine that has gone sour.

Although vinegar can be made from most any mildly sweet liquid, the most miraculous claims for health benefits are those linked to vinegar made from apple cider. So, unless literature specifically says otherwise, references to vinegar usually came to mean apple cider vinegar.

20

Once the ancient world recognized vinegar's value for healing and health, the intentional production of this amazing elixir began. Because vinegar could do so many miraculous things it is not surprising that the souring of apple cider into vinegar was often an elaborate process, with overtones of magic.

Vinegar making was, for thousands of years, more an art form than a science. The physical steps for making vinegar were often augmented with incantations and seemingly superfluous steps.

We now know the complicated recipes of the mediaeval alchemists were not needed. These early recipes owed their success to the accidental infection of their brews with organisms needed for fermentation. It was exposure to air which brought vinegar into being!

WHAT IS VINEGAR?

Technically, vinegar is an acid liquid made from wine, cider, beer (or most any mildly alcoholic beverage) by what is called an "acetous fermentation." What this means, is that alcohol mixes with oxygen in the air. The alcohol then "disappears." (Actually, it is changed into acetic acid and water.)

Acetic acid is what imparts the characteristic tart, puckery taste sensation to vinegar. The acetous fermentation which creates it is due to a tiny microorganism, the vinegar bacillus. This bacterium occurs naturally in the air, everywhere, and is why early vinegar producers were successful.

It was not until 1878, nearly 10,000 years after vinegar making began, that a microbiologist named Hansen correctly explained the chemical process which creates vinegar. He accurately described the three species of vinegar bacilli. These tiny creatures gobble up alcohol and excrete acid. The process where alcohols are changed to acids is called fermentation.

Fermenting is thought by many to endow the end product with a special ability to heal. It is also thought to sharply increase nutritional values. While the primary reason for fermenting foodstuffs was, originally, to keep them from rotting - the result can be better tasting than the original - just ask any pickle fanatic.

Vinegar contains dilute acetic acid. It also has the basic nature and essential nutrients of the original food from which it was made. For example, apple cider vinegar has pectin, beta carotene, and potassium from the apples that were its origin. In addition, it contains generous

Acetous fermentation is how alcoholic liquids, like beer or wine, yield acetic acid.

Don't confuse acetic acid ($C_2H_4O_2$) with vinegar - its often made from wood shavings.

21

portions of health-promoting enzymes and amino acids. These complex protein building blocks are formed during the fermentation process.

Claims for the curative and restorative powers of apple cider vinegar are legendary. Some believe this fabulous liquid is capable of solving the most vexing and tiresome of human afflictions. It has been said to lengthen life and improve hearing, vision, and mental powers.

Devotees claim it will help heartburn, clear up throat irritations, stop hiccups, relieve coughs, deal with diarrhea, and ease asthma.

Over the centuries vinegar became a commonplace remedy for many ills.* It was also found to be useful in cleaning, cooking, and food preservation. Some examples of ancient recipes for health, well-being and sanitation follow:

Ye may ease the rasping of the evening cough by sleeping with the head on a cloth which has been steeped in vinegar.

An aching throat will be eased by rinsing it with water which has been made to blush by the addition of vinegar.

Difficult breathing may be eased by wrapping strips of white cloth, well dampened with vinegar, around the wrists.

Ye may purify the waters of the body by sipping a tonic of goodly vinegar, mixed with clear running water.

Those who sup regularly of the miraculous vinegar will be blessed with a sharp mind for all their life.

Bumps, lumps, and knots of the flesh may be relieved by the timely application of a binding soaked in the best vinegar.

Itching of the flesh may be relieved by the frequent application of vinegar.

Alleviate the discomfort of aching in the lower limbs by wrapping the afflicted area with a cloth wrung out of apple cider vinegar. When the binding begins to dry, renew it with fresh vinegar.

* For more old-time healing ways, see the Order Form for Home Remedies from the Old South.

Make the suffering of one who speweth up their food less grievous by covering the belly with a well washed cloth, well soaked in warm vinegar.

Before scrubbing garments, sprinkle them with vinegar to make the task lighter. This will also make the fabric more agreeable.

Vinegar and salt added to washing water will drive bugs from garden foods.

Saddles and boots may be cleaned with beeswax, soap, oil, and vinegar. Carefully work beeswax into warm vinegar, then add soap and oil. Heat until the ingredients are thoroughly mixed and cool before using.

Soak venison (or other fresh flesh) in vinegar and water before cooking. This will make it palatable and soft for the teeth.

Coarse, sinewy vegetables become more toothsome if, before cooking, they are allowed to rest in water laced with vinegar.

HERB VINEGARS

Those of the ancient world quickly learned to combine vinegar with beneficial plants for maximum medicinal value. Herb vinegars have been in use for thousands of years. Yet, the virtues of healing herbs are only now beginning to be understood by the scientific community. Some examples of vinegars considered to be both healthful and antiseptic follow (see the Cooking With Vinegar chapter for directions on preparing herb vinegars):

DANDELION adds its mild laxative nature to vinegar's natural antiseptic qualities. It also has an anti-inflammatory effect on the intestines. This is an old time remedy for ailments of the pancreas and liver, said to ease jaundice and cirrhosis. It is also a diuretic, and as such is considered useful in lowering blood pressure. (Dandelion is rich in potassium, a mineral some other diuretics pull out of the body.)

MYRRH has long been considered of particular value in maintaining a healthy mouth. Swish this vinegar around in the mouth to hasten healing of sores and to soothe red, swollen gums. This will also sweeten the breath. Ancients used it for treating chest congestion.

SAGE vinegar not only adds its delicate hint of flavoring to meats, it tenderizes them. Splashed into soups and dressings, it serves up a tranquilizer for frazzled nerves.

PEPPERMINT, like all the mints, settles and calms the digestive system. Use a couple of teaspoons of peppermint vinegar, added to a glass of water, to ease stomach cramps, diarrhea, or gas. Add a teaspoon of honey and it is one of the best tasting cures for indigestion. Mix this herb vinegar with others to intensify their flavor and effectiveness.

ROSEMARY, the herb of remembrance, combines with healthy, amino acid laced apple cider vinegar to treat maladies of the head. It boosts the function of mind and memory, relieves tension headaches, and eases dizziness.

EUCALYPTUS is the source of the eucalyptol which makes some cough drops so effective. Steam from vinegar which has absorbed the aromatic oil of this herb helps to clear a stuffy head or a clogged respiratory system. A popular over-the-counter salve for relieving the stiffness and swelling of arthritis and rheumatism carries the distinctive aroma of eucalyptus.

WORMWOOD is quite bitter. This vinegar is best used externally, as a deterrent to fleas and other insects, or applied as a wound dressing. For insect control, sprinkle it liberally onto infested areas of rooms.

RUE was once given as an antidote for poison mushrooms and toadstools, as well as the bite of snakes, spiders, and bees. Bitter, aromatic rue vinegar was once sprinkled about to ward off both witches and contagious diseases.

LAVENDER makes a vinegar that is pleasantly aromatic and useful for fighting off anxiety attacks. The haunting scent of lavender has long been associated with headache relief and calming of stressed nerves.

THYME vinegar is a good addition to meat dishes, as it both flavors and tenderizes. Applied to the body, it acts to deter fungus growth.

SPEARMINT is one of the gentler mints. A bit of spearmint vinegar in a glass of water calms the stomach and digestive system. It also relieves gas and adds a tangy zing to iced tea.

CLOVE vinegar is especially good for stopping vomiting. Its use dates back more than 2,000 years (to China) where it was considered an aphrodisiac.

Eucalyptus is more than just Koala bear food !

Cloves are the dried bud of the clove tree.

24

When herb vinegars are used for medicinal purposes, the usual dose is one to three teaspoons added to a full glass of water. They can also be sprinkled into meat and vegetable dishes or splashed on salads. The very strong vinegars, and the very bitter ones, should be used sparingly, and only for external purposes.

Natural, organic vinegars are not the same as commercially processed and pasteurized products. In its most natural state vinegar is alive with living organisms. These naturally occurring creatures, as well as some enzymes and vitamins are destroyed when vinegar is processed in a high heat process, such as pasteurization. Descriptions of a couple of these little inhabitants of the vinegar barrel follow:

Vinegar eels are frequently found in vinegar. This species of nematode worm is a natural part of many vinegars. These curious creatures can be seen near the surface of a vinegar which has been exposed to air. They resemble tiny thread worms, and are considered a harmless part of vinegar.

Vinegar flies (of the genus Drosophila) lay eggs which hatch out into larvae that live comfortably in vinegar. They thrive on this acid brew, but are not a particularly appetizing addition to vinegar!

Fortunately the vinegaroon - a large scorpion - doesn't live in vinegar! It just smells vinegary!

Chapter Four

Vinegar's Historic Development

As vinegar's virtues became known, its production spread throughout the world. Vinegar's use can be chronicled down through the ages in many different times and cultures. It has been used for everyday cleaning and for specific medical ailments for at least 10,000 years. And sometimes, vinegar can be said to have actually changed the course of history. Some of the more intriguing vinegar uses, as well as some vinegar hints for today, follow.

THE ORIGINAL HOT ROCKS

Was vinegar the world's first bulldozer? Without vinegar, Hannibal's march over the Alps to Rome may not have been possible! The chronicles of this historic march describe the essential role vinegar played in the task of getting Hannibal's elephants over the perilous mountain trails.

Frequently, the tortuous passage across the Alps was too narrow for the huge elephants. Hannibal's solution was for his soldiers to cut tree limbs and stack them around the boulders which blocked their way. Then the limbs were set afire. When the rocks were good and hot, vinegar was poured onto them. This turned the stones soft and crumbly. The soldiers could then chip the rocks away, making a passage for both the troops and elephants.

You may not have an immediate need to relocate a boulder so your elephants can cross a mountain range, but you may want to try some of these ways to ease cleaning chores:

Renew old sponges by washing them in vinegar water, then soaking them overnight in 1 quart of water with 1/4 cup vinegar added to it.

Use vinegar to clean away mineral buildup on metal. Just add 1/4 cup to a quart of water for cleaning metal screen and storm doors and aluminum furniture. Add extra vinegar if your water has a particularly high mineral content.

Eyeglasses will clean up and be free of streaks when wiped down with water to which a splash of vinegar has been added.

Clean and freshen the microwave oven by boiling vinegar water in it. Mix 1/4 cup vinegar and 1 cup water in a small bowl and heat for 5 minutes. This will remove lingering odors and soften baked on food spatters.

Wipe down wood cutting boards with full strength vinegar. It will clean them, cut grease, and absorb odors.

A splash of vinegar added to rinse water will keep glasses from water spotting. It kills germs, too.

Clean and freshen the garbage disposal by running a tray of ice cubes, with 1/2 cup vinegar poured over them, through it once a week.

Make a brass and copper cleaner by combining equal parts of lemon juice and vinegar. Wipe it on with a paper towel, then polish with a soft, dry cloth.

Use vinegar and hay to revitalize iron pans which have rust spots. Fill the pot with hay, add 1/4 cup vinegar and enough water to cover the hay. Boil for 1 hour and wipe the rust away. Rhubarb may be substituted for the hay.

Clean pewter with a paste made of 1 tablespoon salt, 1 tablespoon flour, and enough vinegar to just barely make the mixture wet. Smear it on discolored pewter and allow to dry. Rub or brush the dried paste off, rinse in hot water, and buff dry.

Keep drains clean by pouring in 1/2 cup baking soda, followed by 1/2 cup vinegar. In about 10 minutes, run hot water down the drain. Keep drains odor-free by pouring 1/2 cup vinegar down them once a week.

Wipe all kitchen work surfaces down with full strength white vinegar to clean them and to prevent mold.

Add a generous splash of vinegar to hot water and use it, with a little soap, to disinfect baby's toys. Be sure to rinse well.

Add a cup of vinegar to a bucket of floor washing water for cleaner floors. Or, after the usual washing, rinse floors with clear water, to which a

cup of vinegar has been added. There will be no soap scum to dull the finish.

1/4 cup vinegar added to a load of laundry, along with the usual soap, will brighten colors and make whites sparkle. This will also act as a fabric softener, and inhibit mold and fungus growth. Helps to kill athlete's foot germs on socks, too.

Vinegar is a good addition to the laundry tub when new clothes are being washed for the first time. It will help to eliminate manufacturing chemicals and their odors.

A vinegar rinse will also stop static cling and reduce the amount of lint that settles on clothes. Some laundry stains can be soaked out in equal parts of milk and vinegar.

A little vinegar and salt added to the water you wash leafy green vegetables in will float out bugs and kill germs.

When 1/4 cup linseed oil, 1/8 cup vinegar, and 1/8 cup whiskey are mixed together, they make a nice furniture polish. Dirt seems to disappear as the alcohol evaporates.

Wood scratches can be repaired with vinegar and iodine. Mix equal parts of each in a small dish and apply with an artist's paint brush. Add extra iodine for a deeper color, more vinegar for a lighter color.

A good saddle soap can be made from 1/8 cup liquid soap, 1/8 cup linseed oil, 1/4 cup beeswax, and 1/4 cup vinegar. Warm the beeswax, slowly, in the vinegar. Then add the soap and oil. Keep the mixture warm until it will all mix together smoothly. Then cool until it is solid. To use, rub it onto good leather, then buff to a high shine.

Polish leather with a mixture of 2/3 cup linseed oil, 1/3 cup vinegar, and 1/3 cup water. Beat it all together and apply with a soft cloth. Then buff with a clean rag.

THE MOST EXPENSIVE MEAL EVER

The world's most costly meal began with a glass of vinegar. When asked to think of the most expensive beverage, vinegar may not come immediately to mind. Yet it may take the prize for most expensive drink in history!

Cleopatra, queen of Egypt, made culinary history when she made a wager that she could consume, at a single meal, the value of a million sisterces. To many, it seemed an impossible task. After all, how could anyone eat so much?

Cleopatra was able to consume a meal worth so very much by dropping a million sisterces worth of pearls into a glass of vinegar. Then she set it aside while banquet preparations were made. When the time came to fulfill her wager, she simply drank the dissolved pearls!

Cleopatra won her bet because she knew vinegar was a pretty good solvent. If you do not have an overwhelming urge to dissolve a few thousand dollars worth of pearls, you may want to apply vinegar's remarkable ability in some of the following ways:

Brushes hardened with old, dried-in paint may be softened by boiling them in vinegar. Simply cover them with boiling vinegar and let them stand for 1 hour. Then heat the vinegar and brushes until the vinegar comes to a gentle boil. Simmer for 20 minutes. Rinse well, working the softened paint out of the bristles. For extremely heavy paint encrustations, you may need to repeat the process.

Most any old wood glue can be softened for removal. Simply wet the glued area down with vinegar, and keep it wet overnight. Even some of the newfangled, super-duper, hold-it-all glues can be scraped away if they are soaked overnight in vinegar.

Simmer 1/4 cup vinegar in a pot of water, uncovered, to clear the air of lingering cooking odors. Add 1/2 teaspoon of cinnamon to the water for an extra special air cleaner.

1/2 cup vinegar in dish washing water cuts grease and lets you use less soap.

Make a good metal cleaner by combining 2 tablespoons cream of tartar and enough vinegar to make a paste. Rub it on and let it dry. Wash it off with plain warm water and dry with an old towel. Metal will gleam.

Clean faucets and fixtures with 1/3 cup vinegar and 2/3 cup water. Use it to polish and shine, or brush it into the shower head to remove mineral buildup.

One million sisterces was many years' wages for a workman.

29

Combine 1/4 cup liquid soap, 1/2 cup vinegar, and 2 gallons of water to make a great floor cleaning solution.

Caution: vinegar can dissolve preexisting wax on furniture and floors. Use very small amounts to clean and shine, stronger solutions to remove wax buildup and heavy dirt.

Remove ink stains from clothes by soaking them in milk for 1 hour. Then cover the stain with a paste of vinegar and cornstarch. When the paste dries, wash the garment as usual.

Brass and copper will sparkle and tarnish will melt away if wiped down with 2 tablespoons catsup and 1 tablespoon vinegar. Polish until completely dry with a clean cloth.

Clean and polish soft leather with a vitamin enriched solution. Heat 1/2 cup vinegar to the boiling point. Drop in 3 vitamin E capsules and let stand, undisturbed, until the capsules dissolve. Add 1/2 cup lemon or olive oil and blend well.

Soak or simmer stuck-on food in 2 cups of water and 1/2 cup of vinegar. The food will soften and lift off in a few minutes.

Pewter cleans up easily if rubbed with cabbage leaves. Just wet the leaves in vinegar and dip them in salt before using them to buff the pewter. Be sure to rinse with cool water and dry thoroughly.

Apple cider vinegar removes soap scum from more than just shower walls. Dilute it half and half with water and use it to rub down your body after bathing. It will leave your skin naturally soft, pH balanced, and free of soapy film. It also acts as a natural deodorant.

Nail polish will go on smoother, and stay on longer if you clean your fingernails with white vinegar before applying the polish.

Perspiration stains in clothes will fade if soaked overnight in 3 gallons of water, to which 1/4 cup vinegar has been added. Use full strength vinegar to remove stains caused by berries, fruits, grass, coffee and tea.

Dissolve chewing gum and remove stuck on decals by saturating them with vinegar. If the vinegar is heated, it will work faster.

Clean hairbrushes by soaking them in 2 cups of hot, soapy water, with 1/2 cup vinegar added to it.

Car chrome shines up fast if polished with vinegar!

Keep a dish or two of vinegar sitting around when painting. The vinegar will absorb the paint odors. For a long painting job, fill a bucket with hay and drizzle 1 cup vinegar over it. Let this set for 15 minutes. Then add enough water to cover the hay. This will clear the air and keep the room smelling fresh for a couple of days.

OTHER HISTORIC VINEGAR MOMENTS

The Babylonians, back in 5,000 B.C., fermented the fruits of the date palm. Their vinegar, therefore, was called date vinegar and was credited with having superior healing properties.

You may know that vinegar is mentioned eight times in the Bible. (Four references are in the Old Testament, and four are in the New Testament.) But did you know there was a Vinegar Bible?

One famous version of the Bible is called the Vinegar Bible. In 1717 the Clarendon Press in Oxford, England printed and released a new edition of the scriptures. A mistake was soon discovered. In the top-of-the-page running headline of the 22nd chapter of the book of Luke, the word "vineyard" had been misprinted.

Instead of "vineyard" the printer typeset the word as "vinegar." The edition was quickly dubbed the "Vinegar Bible." And this is the name by which Clarendon's 1717 edition is known today.

Even poets have commented on vinegar. Lord Byron (1788-1824) called vinegar "A sad, sour, sober beverage..."

Well, puckery or not, vinegar's virtuous traits abound. Vinegar cleans by cutting grease. This makes it useful for melting away gummy buildup. It also inhibits mold growth, dissolves mineral accumulations, freshens the air, kills bacteria and slows its regrowth.

Many folk recipes combine vinegar with other household supplies. Chemical company copies of old-time cleaners use synthetic chemicals that are not always as environmentally safe as more natural, organic compounds. Among the more popular substances which have traditionally been used in combination with vinegar are baking soda, borax, chalk, pumice, oil, salt, washing soda, and wax. To vinegar, add:

- Baking soda to absorb odors, deodorize, and as a mild abrasive.
- Borax to disinfect, deodorize, and stop the growth of mold.

It's been at least 10,000 years since the natural souring of wine created the first vinegar.

31

- Chalk for a mild, non abrasive cleaner.
- Oil to preserve and shine.
- Pumice to remove stains or polish surfaces.
- Salt for a mild abrasive.
- Washing soda to cut heavy grease.
- Wax to protect and shine.

PLEASE NOTE: Some ingredients, when added to a vinegar solution, will produce a frothy foam. This is a natural chemical reaction, and is not dangerous in an open container.

**DO NOT SEAL A FOAMING VINEGAR MIXTURE
IN A TIGHTLY CAPPED CONTAINER!**

A collection of useful formulas for cleaning and polishing with vinegar follow:

Make your own kind-to-the-environment air freshener. Put the following into a pump spray bottle: 1 teaspoon baking soda, 1 tablespoon vinegar, and 2 cups of water. After the foaming stops, put on the lid and shake well. Spray this mixture into the air for instant freshness.

Vinegar is an excellent window cleaner. Just mix 1/4 cup vinegar into 1 quart water and put it in a spray bottle. Spray it onto windows and wipe off immediately with clean, soft cloth.

An excellent furniture polish can be made from vinegar and lemon oil. Use 3 parts vinegar to 1 part oil for a light weight polish. (Use 1 part vinegar to 3 parts oil for a heavy duty polish.) An oil and vinegar combination works well for cleaning and polishing. This is because vinegar dissolves and brings up dirt and oil enriches the wood.

Dusting will go much faster if your dust cloth is dampened with a mixture made of half vinegar and half olive oil. Give furniture a nutty fragrance by cleaning with vinegar to which a little olive oil has been added. When the vinegar evaporates, the wood is left clean and beautiful - and smelling good!

Appliances sparkle if cleaned with a vinegar and borax cleaner. Mix 1 teaspoon borax, 1/4 cup vinegar, and 2 cups hot water and put it into a spray bottle. Spray it on greasy smears and wipe off with a cloth or sponge.

Clean brass and copper with 2 teaspoons salt, 1 tablespoon flour, and enough vinegar to make a paste. First, mix the salt and flour together. Next, add vinegar until a thick paste is formed. Then use the paste to scrub the metal, rinse, and buff dry. Add some extra salt for hard jobs, or some extra flour for a softer paste.

Counter tops will shine if wiped down with a mixture of 1 teaspoon liquid soap, 3 tablespoons vinegar, 1/2 teaspoon oil, and 1/2 cup water.

Once a week clean, disinfect, and deodorize wood cutting blocks. Rub them with baking soda. Then spray on full strength vinegar. Let sit for 5 minutes, then rinse in clear water. It will bubble and froth as these two natural chemicals interact.

An excellent toilet cleaner can be made from 1 cup borax and 1 cup vinegar. Pour the vinegar all over the stained area of the toilet. Then sprinkle the borax over the vinegar. Allow it all to soak for 2 hours. Then simply brush and flush.

Clean windows with 1/4 cup cornstarch and 1/4 cup vinegar. Mix well and quickly dab it onto windows. Let it dry and rub off with a clean cloth. Glass will sparkle.

Make your own instant window cleaner! Combine 1/2 teaspoon liquid soap, 1/4 cup vinegar, and 2 cups water. Soak a sponge or small cloth in this mixture, then wring it out. Store the window cloth in a glass jar with a tight fitting lid until needed. Then simply wipe spots and smears from dirty windows. They will clean up without streaks - no mess, no fuss.

Shine and clean painted surfaces with 1 tablespoon cornstarch, 1/4 cup vinegar, and 2 cups hot water. Wipe or spray it on and wipe the paint dry immediately. Rub until it shines.

Preserve leather shoes and clean off dirt by rubbing them with a vinegar based cleaner. Mix together 1 tablespoon vinegar, 1 tablespoon alcohol, 1 teaspoon vegetable oil, and 1/2 teaspoon liquid soap. Wipe it on, then brush until the shoes gleam.

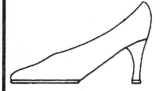

Water scale build up on glass shower doors can be removed with alum and vinegar. Mix 1 teaspoon alum into 1/4 cup vinegar. Wipe it on the glass and scrub with a soft brush. Rinse with lots of water and buff until completely dry. (Alum is aluminum sulfate.)

Soft vinyl surfaces are best cleaned with 1/2 cup vinegar, 2 teaspoons liquid soap, and 1/2 cup water. Use a soft cloth to wipe this mixture onto vinyl furniture, then rinse with clear water and buff dry.

Remove light carpet stains with a paste made of salt and vinegar. Dissolve 2 tablespoons salt in 1/2 cup vinegar. Rub this into carpet stains and let it dry. Vacuum up the residue.

Remove heavy carpet stains with a paste made of salt, borax, and vinegar. Dissolve 2 tablespoons salt and 2 tablespoons borax in 1/2 cup vinegar. Rub this into carpet stains and let it dry. Vacuum up the residue.

Stainless steel cleans up nicely if scrubbed with baking soda which has been dampened with just a little vinegar.

As with all cleaning products, test these old-time solutions to cleaning problems before using them. Always try them out on an inconspicuous area of rugs, upholstery, or clothing.

Cleaners you make yourself cost pennies, instead of the dollars super market cleaners cost. And, what is much more significant, the compounds you put together are safe, natural, and easy on the environment. Commercial equivalents cost more and may be more damaging to the environment.

Using vinegar to clean and disinfect is more than the inexpensive choice from a simpler time. It is the natural choice!*

*For more old-time cleaning ways, see the Order Form for Home Remedies from the Old South.

Chapter Five

Vinegar Making

For thousands of years apple cider vinegar has been made in much the same way. First, cider is made from an assortment of whole, fresh apples: they are washed, chopped, and pressed.

When the sweet apple juice has been collected, it is allowed to age, sealed tightly away from the air. Natural sugars are fermented to produce alcohol. This "hard" cider is then allowed to ferment once again, while left open to the air. This time, the alcohol changes to acid.

Originally, the commercial production of vinegar was a by-product of the wine producer and the brewer. Vinegar brewing, as a separate industry, dates from about the 17th century. First established in France, it quickly spread to other regions.

Vinegar can be made from any liquid containing sugar, if there is enough sugar. Apple juice is one of the oldest fluids used to make vinegar, but grape and date palm use goes back thousands of years. Other popular vinegar sources are: molasses, sorghum, berries, melons, coconuts, honey, maple syrup, potatoes, beets, grains, bananas, and even whey.

Wine vinegar has many of the same nutritional benefits as apple cider vinegar. After all, it begins with naturally ripe, vitamin and mineral packed fruit. Wine vinegar will vary in color, depending on whether it was made from red or white wine. Vinegar's flavor, strength, and nutritional makeup depends on what it is made from. Sometimes "vinegar" is concocted from acetic acid (made from wood), colored with caramel, and then called vinegar. This is incorrect (and illegal) labelling. Acetic acid does not have the food value or aroma of genuine vinegar.

ALEGAR

One of the old-time vinegars made from a grain base is called alegar. Technically, it is a kind of malt vinegar. Malt is barley (or other grain) which

There's even a vinegar tree (Rhus typhina) with acidy berries for vinegar making.

Vinegar made from ale is called alegar.

35

is steeped in water until it germinates, then dried in a kiln for use in brewing. This malt is fermented into an alcoholic beverage called ale. Ale has less hops than beer, so it is both sweeter and lighter in color.

The color of alegar varies from pale gold to rich brown. The intensity of the color depends on how the grain was roasted and dried. Medicated ales have been used for hundreds of years in Europe.

When wine or cider (from grapes or apples) is fermented, the result is called "vine-gar." When ale (from barley or other grain) is fermented, the result is called "ale-gar."

MAKE YOUR OWN VINEGAR

The are as many ways to make vinegar as there are apples, kinds of fruit, and people. If you have never tackled the operation, you may want to begin with the first apple cider vinegar recipe below. Then, experiment with some of the other ways to make vinegar.

Some people use peelings, cores, and windfalls.

Vinegar making requires two separate, distinct fermentations. The first, called alcoholic (or vinous) changes natural sugars to alcohol. The second, called acid (or acetic) changes alcohol to acetic acid. It is important that the first fermenting be completely finished before the second is begun.

You can hurry the first fermentation along by adding a little yeast to the cider, and by keeping it warm. At around 80° the liquids will convert very fast. To speed up the second fermentation, add a little mother-of-vinegar to the mix. And, the more air the mixture gets during this second part of the process, the faster it will convert to vinegar.

Caution: Mother-of-vinegar (it starts the second fermentation) must not get into the liquid until practically all the sugar has been converted to alcohol.

The vinegar bacterium is called an acetobacter.

The vinegar bacterium is present wherever there is air. This is why any wine which is spilled at a winery must be mopped up at once. Bacteria could get started in the wine and sour it all! If a winery makes both wine and vinegar, separate rooms are used for each. And, barrels from vinegar making are never used for storing wine.

APPLE CIDER VINEGAR

Begin by making a good, tart cider. Combine sweet apples for aroma, tart ones for body, and a few crab apples for luck. The more sweet apples you use, the stronger the vinegar will be. This is because the high sugar content of sweet apples produces more alcohol to change into acid. The more tart apples in the mix, the sharper the flavor will be.

Chop the apples and when they turn golden brown, crush them in a cider press. Collect the cider in a glass jug. Never use store-bought apple juice to make vinegar. It contains preservatives, and may have been pasteurized, and so it will not ferment properly!

Next, cap the cider jug with a small balloon. It will expand as carbon dioxide is released, while keeping air away from the mix. When the sugar is all changed to alcohol, it becomes hard cider. This takes 1 to 6 weeks, depending on the temperature and the sugar content of the apples used to make the cider.

Carbon dioxide forms when sugar converts to alcohol.

It is not necessary to add yeast, as wild yeasts are always on apples surfaces and in the air. If a grey foam forms on the top of the cider, it is excess yeast, and is harmless. Just skim it off.

Finally, pour the hard cider into a wide crock, so there is a larger surface area than in a jug. Put a cloth over the top to let in air, while keeping out dust and bugs. Vinegar will be created in a few months.

Wild spores floating in the air will start the fermenting process, but adding mother-of-vinegar to cider will hurry the conversion along. Simply smear a slice of toast with mother and lay it gently on the surface of the cider. Vinegar making works best if the ingredients are kept at around 80°. If the temperature gets much higher, the bacteria needed for fermenting is killed. If the temperature gets much cooler than 80°, the wild spores become dormant.

OTHER OLD APPLE CIDER VINEGAR RECIPES

Put cut up apples in a stone crock and cover them with warm water. Tie a cheesecloth over the top and set in a warm place for 4-6 months. Then strain off the vinegar. For faster action, add a lump of raw bread dough to the crock.

Cider for vinegar should have at least a 10% sugar content.

Let sweet apple cider stand open in a jug for 4-6 weeks and it will become vinegar.

Place apple and peach peelings, and a handful of grape skins, in a widemouthed jar and cover these fruit leavings with cold water. Set in a warm place and add a couple of fresh apple cores every few days. When a scum forms on top, stop adding fresh fruit and let it thicken. When the vinegar is good and strong, strain it through a cheesecloth.

Make vinegar in a special hurry by adding brown sugar, molasses, or yeast to cider.

OTHER VINEGARS

Let a bottle of wine stand, open to the air, in the summer sun. In about 2 weeks it will turn into a nice vinegar. Make winter vinegar by letting wine stand open to the air for about a month.

Put 2 pounds of raisins in a gallon of water and set it in a warm place. In 2 months it will become white wine vinegar. Just strain the vinegar off and bottle it. Make some more vinegar by adding another 1/2 pound of raisins to the dredges and going through the process again.

Make a deeply colored honey vinegar by pouring 1 gallon boiling water over 5 pounds of strained honey. Stir until all of the honey is melted. Then dissolve 1 cake (or package) of yeast in 1 tablespoon of warm water. Spread the yeast on a dry corn cob (or a slice of toast) and float it on the top of the honey-water. Cover the container with a cloth and let it set for 16 days. Take out the corn cob, skim off the scum, and strain the liquid. Now let it stand for a month or so, until it turns into vinegar.

Dark honeys ferment much faster than light ones. Add a cup or two of fruit juice or molasses to honey to speed the change to vinegar.

Because the sugar content of honey varies a lot, you may want to check and see if your water to honey ratio is correct. Do this by dropping an egg into the mixture. It should float in the liquid, with only a small spot showing above the surface. If the egg sinks, add more honey. If the egg floats too high, add more water. This method should assure you that the specific gravity of the mix is about 1.05, the best for making good honey vinegar.

For an extra special, clover-flavored, vinegar add a quart of freshly washed clover blossoms to the honey and water mix. Dandelions add a unique taste to honey vinegar. Just add 3 cups of blossoms to the honey and water. Be sure to strain it before using!

Raspberry vinegar can be prepared by pouring 2 quarts of water over 1 quart of freshly washed red or black raspberries. Cover lightly and let stand overnight. Strain off the liquid and discard the berries. Now prepare 1 more quart of fresh raspberries and pour the same liquid over them. Let this set overnight. Do this for a total of 5 times. Then add 1 pound of sugar to the

Color + flavor of this vinegar depends on the kind of honey used.

A Baume hydrometer will read between 7 and 8.

liquid and stir until it is dissolved. Set the mixture aside, uncovered, for a couple of months. Strain before using.

MOTHER OF VINEGAR

"Mother" (or "mother-of-vinegar") is the term used to describe the mass of sticky scum which forms on top of cider (or other juice) when alcohol turns into vinegar. As the fermentation progresses, mother forms a gummy, stringy, floating lump. Mother is formed by the beneficial bacteria which creates vinegar.

Sometimes mother from a previous batch of vinegar is introduced into another liquid which is in the process of becoming vinegar. This use, as a starter for new vinegars, is why the gooey scum on the top of vinegar is called "mother-of-vinegar."

Sometimes, as mother begins to form, it is disturbed and sinks to the bottom of the container. If it falls into the vinegar it will die, because its oxygen supply is cut off. This dead, slithery blob is called a zoogloea, and is worthless. Mother sinks for two reasons. One, if the vinegar making container is jolted, the film can get wet. This makes it too heavy to float. Two, if too many tiny vinegar eels develop in the liquid, their weight, as they cling to the edges of the developing mother, will weight it down.

Over the ages, traditional vinegar makers developed a deep reverence for the rubbery mass of goo we call mother-of-vinegar. Often, some was saved from a batch of vinegar. Then, it was transferred carefully to new batches of souring wine to work its magic.

Over time, this cultivated mother developed special flavoring abilities. It is still handed down, from generation to generation, and guarded as a secret ingredient in special vinegars. Tiny bits of the old mother are lifted out of one batch of vinegar and put into new batches.

Mother-of-vinegar may also form on stored vinegar supplies. This slime is not particularly appealing, but its presence does not mean the vinegar is spoiled. Skim it off and use the vinegar. While mother may not seem to many to be a particularly appetizing snack, some claim it is endowed with nearly miraculous healing properties. Some old-time mother-of-vinegar remedies follow:

Scoop the stringy mass of mother-of-vinegar from the bottom of a barrel that has held vinegar and save it for treating infectious diseases. Preserve it by mixing it half and half with honey. One small teaspoon of this honey and mother mixture, taken twice a day, gives protection from infectious diseases and parasite infestation.

Dip out a goodly spoonful of the moldy mother-of-vinegar from the top of a vinegar barrel and eat it very slowly. This healthy slime will relieve joint pains and headaches caused by infections.

Rashes caused by infections may be made to go away by nibbling on the mother which floats on a good vinegar. And, a bit of mother-of-vinegar, taken each day, prevents most infectious diseases.

Take a bite or two of mother-of-vinegar, morning and evening. It will keep grievous germs and nasty parasites away from the body.

Grow your own mother-of-vinegar by combining 1 cup of vinegar and 1 cup of fresh cider. Let this set, open to the air, for a few days (or weeks, depending on the temperature). The scum which forms on the surface is mother-of-vinegar.

HOW STRONG IS YOUR HOMEMADE VINEGAR?

Homemade vinegars can vary. What follows is one way to determine the percent of acid in a batch of vinegar. You will need 1/2 cup water and 2 teaspoons baking soda, mixed together. Plus, 1/4 cup of the water in which a head of red cabbage was cooked.

A wine testing kit will also check the acidity of vinegar.

1.   Put 1/2 cup water into each of 2 clear glasses.

2.   Add 1/8 cup cabbage water to each glass.

3.   Use a glass dropper to put 7 drops of commercial vinegar into one glass of the cabbage flavored water.

4.   Put 20 drops of the soda water into the same glass and stir well (stir with a plastic spoon, not metal). The water will turn blue.

5.   Now mix 7 drops of your vinegar into the second glass of the cabbage flavored water.

6.   Add baking soda water to your vinegar (and cabbage water), 1 drop at a time. Stir after each drop. Count the drops.

7.   When the color of your vinegar water turns the same shade of blue as the commercial vinegar water, the acid content of the two glasses will match.

Determining vinegar's strength this way is called titration!

8.   To find the percent of acid in your vinegar, divide the number of drops of soda water you added to it by 4. For example, if you added 20 drops of soda water to your vinegar, divide by 4 and find that the acid content is 5%. (The same as most commercial vinegars.) The more soda water it takes to make your vinegar match the color of the commercial vinegar you are using as a control, the stronger your vinegar is.

Chapter Six

In A Pickle And Proud Of It!

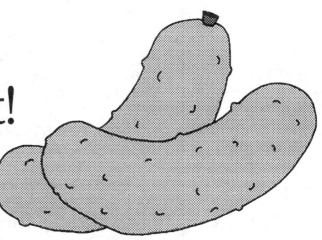

It's the law: if the label says pickled, then the product must be put up in vinegar!

Our world would be very different without vinegar's lively flavor to perk up humdrum foods. Each year, Americans use hundreds of millions of gallons of vinegar. It is used alone, in pickling, and in innumerable condiments.

The best vinegars begin with healthful, natural foods. Inexpensive vinegar, intended for industrial use, is sometimes fraudulently sold for preserving foods.

Cheap imitations are made from liquid sulfite waste from paper mills and acids from petrochemical sources such as oil, coal, and natural gas. Because grain and spirit vinegar is so much cheaper than food-grade vinegar (such as apple cider vinegar) there is a lot of financial incentive for businesses to use it.

There are also differences in the way taxes and import duties treat different grades of vinegar. Quality vinegar, from expensive food-base sources such as fruit juices, honey, maple syrup, apples, grapes, or even sugar cane or corn rates a higher tax.

Different tax treatment dates way back in time. In England, the Revenue Acts established during the reign of Charles II charged different duties on beer and on vinegar- beer.

Charles II reigned in the mid 1600's!

Besides the differences in nutritional values, grain and spirit vinegars do not compare in taste to good, high-quality vinegars. A quality vinegar has a sour taste, without being bitter.

Sour tastes are one of the sensations the body is most able to detect. The sensitive sides of the tongue (the area where sour is registered) can detect one sour part in 130,000. But it is even more sensitive to bitter flavors. The tongue can detect one bitter part out of 2 billion. This sensitivity is a safety measure, to alert the body to poisons. It also makes cheap vinegars unpleasant to the tongue.

Good, sour, acidy vinegar causes saliva to flow. This increases our ability to taste and enjoy other foods. It also aids digestion.

Pickling is one of the most basic, and easiest ways to preserve edibles. It works by increasing food's acidity. Expect a batch of pickled vegetables to last a month or two in the refrigerator. Or, over a year if they are canned.

Because pickles are already partially preserved, they do not have to be canned in a pressure cooker. A boiling water bath provides enough heat to seal and sterilize them. Care does need to be taken in choosing containers. The high acid content reacts with some metals, such as aluminum and iron. It is better to use enamel, glass, or stainless steel pans.

Even the water which is combined with the vinegar can affect the quality of the pickled food. Water high in iron or sulfur will darken foods. Be sure food to be preserved is of high quality, not bruised or damaged.

PERSONALIZING TASTE

Everyone has their own idea of what the perfect pickle should taste like. There are several things you can do to adjust the taste: vary the kind of vinegar used, add or delete sugar, or change the spices.

There are some things you do not want to do in your quest for preserving the perfect pickle. Do not combat vinegar's tartness by diluting the vinegar excessively. This will lower the acid content of the mixture and could result in spoiled pickles.

It is better to mask tartness by adding extra sugar. Since sugar helps to preserve the food, doing this will not create a risk of spoilage. Use brown sugar and the entire batch will change to a darker color. Use honey and the flavor will be heavy and rich.

The salt used for pickling should always be "pickling salt" or "kosher salt." They are both free of the iodine and starch often found in table salt. Iodine in the salt will darken the pickles, and the starchy anticaking additives in table salt will cause the liquid to be cloudy.

Make simple cucumber pickles, or be creative and preserve eggplant, cauliflower, carrots, beans, onions, okra, Brussels sprouts, squash, beets, or asparagus. Even fruits can be pickled.

Flavor your mix with oregano, bay, red pepper, turmeric, mustard seeds or dry mustard, garlic, basil, dill, peppercorns, bell peppers, hot peppers, onions, or garlic.

BASIC PICKLING

Always use firm, young veggies, because they make the crunchiest pickled food. And never store cucumbers for pickling in the refrigerator. They deteriorate if stored below 50°.

For best taste, cut off the blossom ends (opposite end from the stem) of cucumbers. There are concentrated enzymes in the flowering end of the cucumber and they can soften pickles.

Never boil vinegar for pickles any longer than absolutely necessary. Acetic acid evaporates at boiling temperatures, leaving a vinegar which is too weak to do a good job of preserving.

Slice lots of cucumbers and a few onions. Arrange them in a crock, in layers. Sprinkle salt over each layer. Add very cold water and let them set and become very crisp. While the cucumbers and onions soak, mix sugar, vinegar, and spices in an enamel pan. Bring the liquid to a boil and immediately remove from the heat. Drain the brine off the cucumbers and onions. Add the pickles to the hot spiced vinegar. Put the mixture into clean jars and boil. When cool, set the jars away for a few weeks before beginning to use the pickles.

And remember, pickles pick up the flavor of whatever they are marinated in. This is what gives them their flavor. Traditionally, pickled foods are served at the beginning of a meal because they stimulate the flow of saliva and gastric juices. This makes other foods taste better.

Exact amounts of spices, salt, sugar, and vinegar will depend on your own judgement. What tastes great to one person will be too tart, or too sweet, or too garlicy to another. Do not be afraid to experiment. Some pickling recipes are included in the Cooking With Vinegar chapter.

You can pickle a peck of Hot peppers in a flash.

Pickled foods are sturdy, able to withstand a lot of variation in the way they are processed. However, occasionally things do go wrong. The finished product is not perfect. Too strong or too weak a vinegar solution, or the wrong balance of sugar or salt can result in pickles that are not crisp and crunchy. Contact with minerals can cause pickles to turn unusual colors. Use the following information to identify the cause of pickling problems.

WHAT CAN GO WRONG WITH PICKLED FOODS?

If:	Pickles will be:
Pickling solution (vinegar) is too strong	Tough
Brine is too weak	Soft
Table salt is used (it contains starch)	Cloudy
Pickling solution is too strong	Shriveled
Too much sugar	Shriveled
Too much salt	Tough
Cucumbers are old	Hollow
Cooked in a copper kettle	Off Color
Insufficient time in brine solution	Slippery
Water has a high mineral content	Off color
Cooked too long	Mushy

Chapter Seven

Cooking With Vinegar

A splash of protein, a dash of carbohydrate, and lots of vitamins and minerals - that's vinegar! A vinegary person is thought of as one who is ill-natured and sour. A vinegary food is apt to be one which has been changed from ordinary to gourmet. Vinegar's unique flavor perks up the taste of foods and keeps them safe from bacteria. Vinegar comes in dozens of kinds and flavors. Some ways to make and use flavored vinegars follow, along with a few other interesting vinegar facts and recipes:

Vinegar's acid softens muscle fiber in meat so it is tenderized. It also works on fish such as salmon, and on lobster, oysters, fruits, and vegetables.

Vinegar helps digest tough cellulose, so use it on coarse, fibrous, or stringy cooked vegetables such as beets, cabbage, spinach, lettuce, and celery. Sprinkle it on raw vegetables such as cucumbers, kale, lettuce, carrots, and broccoli.

Splash vinegar into bean soups, or use herb vinegar on pasta or bean salads to give robust flavor without salt.

Because meat fiber is broken down and tenderized by vinegar, less expensive cuts can be used in most recipes. They are healthier, since these are the cuts with the least fat.

Unless directions indicate otherwise, all flavored vinegars are made by adding flavoring agents to apple cider vinegar and allowing it to age.

Hot Pepper Vinegar
Add 1/2 ounce cayenne pepper to 1 pint of vinegar. Shake every other day for 2 weeks. Strain before using.

Spicy Vinegar

1 quart vinegar	1 teaspoon cloves
1/2 cup sugar	1 teaspoon salt
1 tablespoon cinnamon	4 tablespoons grated horseradish
1 teaspoon allspice	2 tablespoons celery seed
1 tablespoon mustard	

Combine all ingredients and bring to a boil. Pour over pickles or sliced, cooked beets.

Celery Vinegar

1 teaspoon salt
2 cups chopped celery
1 quart vinegar

Boil for 3 minutes and seal it all in a glass jar for 3 weeks. Strain and use.

Chili Vinegar

Add 3 ounces chopped chilies to a quart of vinegar. Cap for 2 weeks and strain. For a supper hot vinegar, increase steeping time.

Cucumber-Onion Vinegar

Slice very thin, 2 pickling cucumbers and 1 small onion. Add 1 pint boiling vinegar, 1 teaspoon salt and a dash of white pepper. Seal into a glass jar for 5 weeks and then strain. Allow sediment to settle and pour into a clean bottle and cap. Onion may be left out for a light vinegar that is especially good on fruit.

Horseradish Vinegar

Grate 1/4 cup horseradish into a quart of boiling vinegar. Seal for 3 days and then strain out the horseradish. Or, prepare an easy vinegar by simply putting a few large pieces of fresh horseradish in a bottle of vinegar. After 2 weeks, begin using the vinegar, without removing the horseradish. It will increase in strength over time.

Onion Vinegar

Peel three small onions and drop them, whole, into 1 quart vinegar. Wait 3 weeks. Remove the onions and use the vinegar, very sparingly. A few drops will be enough to season most foods.

Nasturtium Vinegar

1 quart nasturtium flowers
2 cloves garlic
1 quart vinegar

Combine and age for 6 weeks. Strain and use. May be improved by adding 2 peeled cloves of garlic.

Flower Power Vinegar

Add a flower scent to any vinegar by dropping in a few drops of scented oil. Or, add 1/2 cup of strong herb tea to a quart of vinegar.

Strawberry Vinegar

Crush 1 quart of strawberries into 1 quart of vinegar. Let set for 2 days, lightly covered; strain through doubled cheesecloth and discard the berries. Pour the same vinegar over another quart of berries and mash them. After 2 more days, strain off the vinegar and add 2 pounds of sugar. Boil for 10 minutes. A couple of tablespoons of this vinegar in a glass of water is cooling and refreshing.

Tarragon Vinegar

Put 1/4 cup tarragon leaves in a pint bottle of vinegar and let set for 8 weeks. Use on cooked and raw vegetables.

Garlic Lover's Vinegar

Separate and peel all the cloves of a large garlic bulb. Put them in a quart of vinegar and allow to steep for 2 weeks. Strain off the vinegar and discard the garlic. Only a few drops are needed in most dishes.

Mint Vinegar

Stuff a bottle full of mint leaves. Then fill the bottle with hot vinegar, cap and let set for 6 weeks. Strain and use with meats or in cool drinks.

Meat Flavoring Vinegar

1	large grated onion	1	tablespoon dry mustard
3	red peppers, chopped fine	1	teaspoon turmeric
2	tablespoons brown sugar	1	teaspoon pepper
1	tablespoon celery seed	1/2	teaspoon salt

Stir all ingredients into a quart of vinegar. Let age for 3 weeks. 2 tablespoons of this will flavor and color a stew or gravy.

Vinegar Fish Broth

2	quarts cold water	3	small cut up carrots
1	cup vinegar	2	small sliced onions
1	tablespoon salt	4	thyme leaves

Bring the water to a boil in a large fish kettle. Add the rest of the ingredients and 5 pounds of large pieces of salmon or trout. Simmer gently, until the fish is barely tender. Add a handful of peppercorns and a few sprigs of parsley.

All kinds of fish are easier to scale if they are rubbed with vinegar and allowed to set for 5 minutes before scaling.

Stuffed Peppers
Stuff large green peppers with cabbage slaw and stack in a stone crock. Cover with vinegar and age 4 weeks before using.

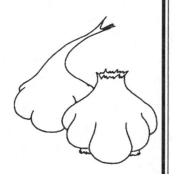

Vinaigrette
1/2	teaspoon salt
1/2	teaspoon paprika
1/8	teaspoon pepper
1/2	cup apple cider vinegar
1/2	cup olive oil
1	tablespoon minced pickles
1	tablespoon grated green pepper
1	tablespoon chopped parsley
1	tablespoon dry mustard
1	tablespoon sugar
1	tablespoon tarragon vinegar

Mix well and chill the vinaigrette. Serve with cold meats or heat it and pour over broccoli, artichokes, or asparagus. A vinegar sauce on vegetables and meats is a nice touch for hot summer days.

If vinaigrettes are made with high quality vinegar, you can use more vinegar and less oil.

Best French Dressing
Soak a split clove of garlic for at least 30 minutes in 1 cup of vinegar. Discard the garlic (or add it to soup). Mix in 1 tablespoon each of dry mustard and sugar; 1 teaspoon each of salt and paprika. Add 1 1/2 cups of salad oil and mix well. Use flavored vinegars to vary the taste.

Spiced Mushrooms
1	pound fresh mushrooms.	1	tablespoon olive oil
1/2	cup apple cider vinegar	1	tablespoon ginger
1	teaspoon soy sauce	3	cloves garlic, peeled
1	teaspoon hot pepper sauce		and chopped

Blanch mushrooms in boiling water for 2 minutes, drain and pat dry. Put all ingredients into a jar with a tight lid and refrigerate overnight. Pile these mushrooms on spinach leaves and serve with hot garlic toast.

Vinegar Salad

1/2 cup salad dressing
1/2 cup apple cider vinegar
1 tablespoon sugar
1 cup raisins

1/2 lb. bacon, cooked crisp and crumbled
1 cup sunflower kernels
2 cups chopped and blanched broccoli
half a head of lettuce

Mix the salad dressing, sugar, and vinegar together and drizzle over torn lettuce, raisins, bacon, sunflower kernels and broccoli.

Cherry-Pineapple Vinegar Cake

1 cup milk
3 tablespoons vinegar
1 teaspoon soda
3/4 lb. flour
3/4 cup butter

3/4 cup brown sugar
1 teaspoon allspice
1/2 lb. candied cherries
1/2 lb. candied pineapple

Stir the vinegar into the milk, add the soda and stir briskly. Cream butter, sugar, and flour together and add the fruit and allspice. Fold in the milk and beat well. Bake in a well greased pan at 350° for 1 hour.

Easiest Vinegar Pie Crust

1 1/3 cup flour
1/2 teaspoon salt
2 tablespoons sugar

1 tablespoon vinegar
1/3 cup oil
2 tablespoons water

Put all ingredients in a pie pan and stir with a fork until the flour is barely moist. Use the fingers to press and smooth the dough onto the sides and bottom of the pie pan, forming a fluted edge along the top. Prick with a fork and bake at 350° until lightly browned. (Or add filling and bake.)

About Vinegars . . . . .

. . . . . All vinegars are not created equal.

Vinegar made from wood shavings cannot be expected to have the same natural balance of healthful vitamins and minerals as vinegar made from apples. And, vinegar made from only cores and peelings cannot be expected to have the nutritional goodness of vinegar made from whole apples. The very best, most wholesome apple cider vinegar is made from apples without pesticide residue on them. These apples will contain an abundance of minerals, because they were grown on rich, fertile soil.

A first class apple cider vinegar is packed full of healthy enzymes, amino acids, vitamins and minerals. This is only true if it has been produced with care, from whole, good quality apples -- that have not been treated with toxic chemicals.

ORGANIC - WHAT DOES IT MEAN?

It seems as if every time we turn around we hear or see something which carries the 'organic' label. Ever wonder, exactly, what it means? Well, somtimes it means a lot. Other times it means very little.

One way to be certain an apple cider vinegar is free of harmful chemicals is to make sure that both the apples it was made from -- and the method of processing it -- are biologically sound. Companies which produce this type of product usually have an outside organization inspect all phases of production and issue an 'organically grown and processed' certificate.

WHAT CAN GO WRONG?

Sometimes, in their haste to market a vinegar, companies process apples with chemicals that speed up the fermentation process. Or, to cut costs, windfalls and apple by-products (such as cores and peels) take the place of whole fruit.

Many vinegars are subjected to excessive heat and have preservatives and clarifying agents added to them. These procedures may make a 'pretty' product, but they can sacrifice some of the healthy goodness which is present in an organically produced vinegar.

WHY IS 'ORGANIC' IMPORTANT?

Everyone experiences the wear and tear of time on their bodies. Scientists tell us that much of what we call aging is damage caused by free radicals. They bounce through our bodies, damaging cells and causing them to mutate. If we eat the right kinds of wholesome foods many free radicals are absorbed. This minimizes the damage. The better job we do of providing our bodies with the building blocks of a healthful being, the better it can retain the vitality and energy of youth.

Apples contain the building blocks for a healthy being. Pure, unfiltered, apple cider vinegar combines the natural goodness of apples with amino acids and enzymes created in the fermentation process. They remain in the vinegar if it is not filtered, overheated, pasteurized, or over-processed.

HOW TO PICK A VINEGAR

Good apple cider vinegar is made by giving meticulous attention to producing a consistent, high quality product. It is not diluted with water, and can take a full four to six weeks to produce.

For a high quality product, check that the apples were organically grown, on soil in an area with a high mineral content (such as the northern area of the U.S.). It should be made of table-grade apples, not merely windfalls, peels or cores. There should be third party monitoring of its organic status.

The best vinegar is aged in wood barrels, not plastic or metal ones. Pectin and apple residues have not been filtered out, so it contains a host of trace nutrients. And, the apples it is made from have been thoroughly washed to remove soil bacteria that could get into the finished product. This kind of vinegar will be full-flavored and have a strong apple aroma. It will not be a washed out, overly bland or puckery concoction.

VINEGAR TEST: SHAKE IT UP!
Check for sediment at the bottom of the vinegar bottle. If there is none, the very best part has probably been filtered out.

FINALLY

If you are sensitive to food additives...
If you don't want possibly toxic chemicals added to your diet....
If you are serious about protecting your health....
If you appreciate the full taste and flavor of a quality product...
Or if you just want to treat yourself to something special that's not fattening -- and is actually good for you -- try a good, organically produced, apple cider vinegar!

Life is a natural process. Your vinegar should be natural, too.

If you expect vinegar to aid health, for goodness sake, use the good stuff!

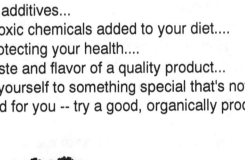

51

Chapter Eight

What's New?

Vinegar is a familiar ingredient in all sorts of condiments. Tomato ketchup, alone, uses up 10% of all the vinegar made in North America. Vinegar also adds its zip to salad dressing, mayonnaise, and a variety of sauces. It is used to make pickles and to preserve foods ranging from beets to eggs to fish. But of even more importance is vinegar's medicinal use. It is useful as an antibiotic, an antiseptic, and as a nutritional supplement.

Vinegar is not the only nonprescription health enhancer making news in the 90s. All of alternative medicine is "going mainstream," according to a recent headline in USA TODAY. One third of the population uses some form of alternative medicine. It accounts for 425 million visits, each year, to alternative care providers. That's more than 35 million more visits than all those to family doctors and internists, combined.

The #1 reason for adults to visit the doctor is back pain!

This non-traditional care accounted for $13.7 billion worth of scarce health care dollars. This is particularly significant when taken with the fact that almost all of the cost of alternative medical care must be paid for as an out-of-pocket expense by the consumer. Most insurance does not cover it. Of growing concern to traditional health care professionals is the fact that 72% of those using alternative health care services do not tell their doctors about it.

The National Institutes of Health has responded to this new interest in old medicine. It recently established, for the first time ever, an Office of Alternative Medicine. The new agency's first budget, of $2 million, is almost entirely dedicated to exploring the value of old-time, traditional, low-tech health remedies.

The government's rush to validate traditional remedies is partly driven by a desire to cut skyrocketing costs. After all, old remedies are almost always low-tech, low-cost solutions to the common maladies of mankind.

Devotees of apple cider vinegar are not surprised to hear that improved nutrition is emerging as a major factor in controlling health care costs. It also is a large step forward in increasing the quality of life for many people.

Much new evidence suggests diet supplements may help much more than many doctors have been willing to believe in the past. A recent CBS television special featured the network's resident medical specialist. He guided researchers through a survey of the shelves of health food stores. A laboratory then analyzed the contents of several bottles of popular food supplements.

The lab's results were shocking. Many bottles did not contain the amount of nutrient buyers were led to believe they contained. CBS's conclusion was that consumers cannot count on vitamin and other dietary supplement bottles containing what the labels say they contain.

This report, and others like it, make taking simple, naturally healthy apple cider vinegar look better and better! Some of the newest medical information about vinegar use follows:

DON'T SWIM WITHOUT IT!

Jellyfish stings are no trivial matter. They can easily land a swimmer in the hospital. The Medical Journal of Australia now recommends immediate dousing of fresh stings with vinegar, considering it "...an essential part of the first aid treatment for ... jellyfish stings."

The Massachusetts College of Pharmacy and Allied Health Sciences seconds this approach, noting that without immediate treatment jellyfish and Portuguese man-of-war stings can cause nausea, headache, chills, or even cardiovascular collapse and death. Yet, they add, "Venom can be inactivated with ... vinegar.

Traditionally, vinegar has been the remedy of choice for treating all sorts of stings and bites. Stings of bees, wasps, jellyfish, and many other bothersome critters can be eased by soaking the hurting area in full-strength vinegar. For best results the vinegar should be applied immediately after an encounter with any of these pesky creatures.

DOCTORS RECOMMEND IT FOR EARS

Grandmother said putting diluted vinegar in the ears would ward off infection. Now medical authorities have confirmed her wisdom. The American Academy of Otolaryngology (head and neck surgery) suggests using a mixture of vinegar and alcohol to prevent "swimmer's ear."

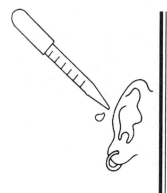

Infections, as well as plain old itchy ears, are a common complaint of swimmers. Doctors specializing in treating these ailments now recommend using vinegar as a preventive. Simply dilute vinegar half and half with boiled water and use to rinse out the ears after each swim. For a more drying solution, mix vinegar half and half with alcohol. This helps to prevent both bacterial and fungus growths.

The Journal of ET Nursing reports vinegar is so good for the skin it is being used to treat some after-urinary-surgery skin complications. When urine, which is often alkaline, leaks onto delicate skin surfaces, it can irritate or even burn sensitive skin. Vinegar's pH balance is very close to that of healthy skin. And so, vinegar compresses, applied to the skin, help restore its natural acid condition, neutralize leaking urine, and promote healing.

MICROBES & PARASITES DESTROYED BY VINEGAR

A recent university test on agents which can kill microbes said: "...(vinegar) was found to be the most effective agent used, which completely inhibited the growth of the test organism..."

Another report addresses vinegar's killer action on bacteria on vegetables intended for eating: "... vinegar solution for 15 minutes exerted pronounced bactericidal effect against this organism."

In Ethiopia, Addis Abba University reports vinegar is being tested as an agent to kill food-borne parasites. Early results show vinegar does a faster job of destroying the parasites than any of the other test mediums!

VINEGAR FOR ARTHRITIS

The Journal of the American Dietetic Association, while remaining extremely conservative in recommending alternative medical solutions, has proposed the possibility that there is room for both approaches to health. An article on arthritis suggested nutrition professionals should be "nonjudgmental" in relating to patients using unconventional therapies (such as apple cider vinegar) for relief of the discomfort of arthritis.

Meanwhile, a national newspaper reports vinegar and fruit juice can beat arthritis pain. Vinegar is sometimes prescribed for those suffering from arthritis or rheumatism, because it is rich in potassium. And potassium, says a University of California doctor, helps relieve arthritis type pain.

According to the Wall Street Journal, vinegar is being combined with apple and grape juices to produce one of the hottest selling sports drinks on the market. This "new" drink is reputed to ease arthritis pain, improve blood circulation, and tackle heart disease. 1 million jugs of this liquid, at $6 a bottle, are expected to be sold this year. Its secret ingredient? Apple cider vinegar!

CANCER DETECTION JUST GOT BETTER

Western Michigan University reports early test results which indicate vinegar can be used to increase the accuracy of conventional tests for cervical cancer. Adding the new vinegar-based test to the standard Pap test allows medical personnel to "...detect women at risk for cervical cancer who would not have been detected by the Pap test alone." The vinegar test is simple for technicians, low-cost, non-invasive, and safe for the patient.

CAN VINEGAR PREVENT ULCERS?

Will new scientific research prove vinegar can prevent stomach ulcers caused by alcohol? Early studies, printed in the Japanese Journal of Pharmacology, indicate vinegar may cause the gastric system to secrete a natural stomach protective. This natural defensive action seems to protect the stomach from alcohol-induced damage. Most surprising of all, a vinegar solution as mild as a 1% concentration appears to offer 95.8% protection from these ulcers.

Much more research work needs to be done before the medical community is ready to recommend using vinegar this way. Results have been noted only in very controlled test situations, so far. Further testing needs to be done to determine exactly how vinegar works to build up the stomach's ability to protect itself from damage that can be done by excess alcohol. But there is a definite possibility this may be a future ulcer preventative!

VINEGAR CAN BE DANGEROUS!

Lead can be a serious health danger. Latest studies indicate vinegar can increase the possibility of foods being contaminated with lead. Many soft plastic bread wrappers have been found to have labels painted on with lead based paints.

If vinegar, or foods drenched in it, are stored in these bags lead could very well leach out into the food. This can happen in as little as 10 minutes. The danger of vinegar leaching lead into food only occurs if the plastic bread wrappers are turned inside out, with the paint side next to the food.

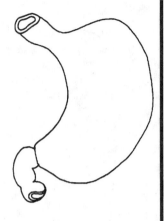

Some individuals report temporary stomach distress when vinegar is taken frequently. This is particularly a problem when vinegar (or vinegar-water) is taken on an empty stomach. Taking vinegar with honey may help to ease this problem.

Dental researchers have reported that excess use of vinegar (and other high acid liquids such as carbonated beverages and fruit juices) can cause loss of tooth enamel. The reports concentrate on damage done to the teeth of relatively young people, but caution should be exercised by anyone using vinegar on a regular basis. You may want to consider drinking your daily vinegar tonic through a straw, to limit its exposure to tooth enamel.

THEN AGAIN, MAYBE ITS NOT SO BAD!

The British Dental Journal carried a study which says vinegary snack foods are among the least harmful to teeth! The study found vinegar crisps (along with peanuts) were less detrimental to teeth than high carbohydrate (sugary) snacks.

VINEGAR CAN BE FUN!

A Louisiana firm now produces some very special pickles. Called Upside-Down Cajun Brand Pickles, they come in rather ordinary looking glass jars. But, the jar labels are applied upside-down. This means, when the label is right-side-up, the lid is at the bottom. Supposedly, keeping pickle jars up-side-down keeps the pickles fresher!

A NEW GENERATION OF VINEGAR

Until recently all vinegar was pretty much the same strength. Now Heinz U.S.A. has introduced a vinegar intended just for cleaning. It is twice as strong as conventional vinegar. This is a white vinegar, not apple cider vinegar. It promises to make cleaning and disinfecting with vinegar easier.

Note: The new Heinz vinegar is meant to be used for cleaning, not for cooking or as a diet supplement.

REFERENCES

ABALAN, F. Med Hypoth 15: 385, 1984.

"ACADEMY Offers Tips to Avoid Swimmers Ear." American Academy of Otolaryngology-Head and Neck Surgery

ALLGEIER, R.J., G.B. Nickol, and H.A. Conner. "Vinegar: History and Development." Part I. [Research Dept. of] U.S. Industrial Chemicals Co. pp. VI-2VI-4.

ALLGEIER, R.J., G.B. Nickol, and H.A. Conner. "Vinegar: History and Development." Part II. [Research Dept. of] U.S. Industrial Chemicals Co.

ANDERSON, J.W., W.J.L. Lin Chen. American Journal of Clinical Nutrition 32(2), 1979. pp. 346-363.

"ASK the Experts." University of California, Berkeley Wellness Letter. Oct. 1990: 8.

"ASSUMING Stomach Atrophy, Elderly Should Take Calcium with Meals." Geriatrics 6 June 1986: 19.

BEADNELL, C.E., T.A. Rider, J.A. Williamson, and P.J. Fender. Medical Journal of Australia 4 May 1992: 655-8.

BELLEME, John. East West Aug 1990: 30(6).

BLOCK, Gladys, Blossom Patterson, and Amy Subar. Nutrition and Cancer 18(1): 1-31.

BLOT, William J., Jun-Yao Li, Phillip R. Taylor, Wande Guo, Sandford Davsey, Guo-Qing Wang, Chung S. Yang Su-Fang Zheng, Mitchell Gail, Guang-Yi Li, Yu Yu, Buo-qi Liu, Joseph Tangrea, Yu-hai Sun, Fusheng Liu, Joseph F. Fraumeni, Jr., You-Hui Zhang, Bing Li. Journal of National Cancer Institute 15 Sept 1993: 1483-1492.

BRAGG, Paul C., ND., Ph.D. [Biochemist], and Patricia Bragg, ND., Ph.D. Apple Cider Vinegar Health System. California: Health Science. pp. 4-5, 26-27.

"Bright Ideas." regarding Michael Brimhall of the Peter Coppola Salon in New York City. Parade Magazine 30 May 1993: 7.

BURKITT, D.P., A.R.P. Walker, and N.S. Painter. Journal of the American Medical Association 229, 1974. pp. 1068-1074.

CANET, Merilyn. British Dental Journal p. 158.

"CIDER." The Encyclopedia Britannica. London: Encyclopedia Britannica Company, Ltd., . p. 700.

DAVIS, A. Let's Cook It Right. New York: New American Library, 1970.

DELANEY, Lisa and Stephanie Ebbert. Prevention Jan 1992: 33(8).

DELHEY, Diane M., MS, RD, Ellen J. Anderson, MS, RD, and Susan H. Laramee, MS, RD. Journal of the American Dietetic Association October 1989: 1448(4).

DE VINCENZI, M., F. Castriotta, S. DiFolco, A. Dracos, M. Magliola, R. Mattei, I. Purificato, A. Stacchini, P. Stacchini, and V. Silano. Food Additives & Containments April-June 1987: 161-218.

"DIETARY Fibre: Effects on Plasma and Biliary Lipids in Men." in Medical Aspects of Dietary Fibre, Spiller, G.A., Kay, R.M., eds., Plenum Press, N.Y. 1980. p. 153.

"DIETARY Supplements Reduce Cancer Deaths in China." Journal of the National Cancer Institute 15 Sept 1993: 1448-1449.

"ELDERLY Are Advised to Take Calcium with Meals." American Family Physician 34 #3: 188.

ERSHOFF, B.H. and W.E. Marshall. Journal of Food Science 40, 1975.

ERSHOFF, B.H. Journal of Food Science 41, 1976. p. 949.

FACKLEMAN, K.A. Science News 25 Sept 1993: 144.

FASANELLA, R.M. Ophthalmic Surgery Feb 1991.

FENNER, P.J., P.F. Fitzpatrick, R.J. Hartwick, and R. Skinner. Medical Journal of Australia 9-23 Dec 1985: 550-1.

GELB, Barbara Levine. The Dictionary of Food And What's in it for You. New York: Paddington Press, 1986. pp. 150, 244.

GHEBREKIDAN, H. " Ethiopian Medical Journal Jan 1992: 23-31.

GRAY, Gregory E., MD, PhD. Journal of American Dietetic Association Dec 1989: 1795-1802.

HAAS, Elson M., M.D. Staying Healthy with Nutrition-The Complete Guide to Diet and Nutritional Medicine. California: Celestial Arts, 1992. p. 299-300, 349.

HADFIELD, L.C., L.P. Beard, and T.K. Leonard-Green. Journal of the American Dietetic Association Dec 1989: 1810-1.

HARDINGE, M.G., M.D., PhD, A.C. Chambers, BA, H. Crooks, BS., and Frederick J. Stare, M.D., PhD. American Journal of Clinical Nutrition 6(5), 1958. pp. 523-525.

HARTLEY, Tom. Business First of Buffalo 4 March 1991: 1,18.

HENDLER, Sheldon Saul, M.D., PhD. The Complete Guide to Anti-Aging Nutrients. New York: Simon & Schuster, 1985. pp. 27, 69-71, 104-106, 144-146, 170, 182-183, l94-195.

HENDLER, Sheldon Saul, M.D., PhD. The Purification Prescription. New York: William Morrison & Co., 1991. p. 56.

HILLS, M. Curring Arthritis-the Drug-Free Way. London: Sheldon, 1985.

"HONEY." Encyclopedia Britannica. 1980 ed.

HUMPHREYS, Dr. Patricia. Countryside & Small Stock Journal May-June 1988: 13-14.

HYLTON, William H., ed. The Rodale Herb Book. Pennsylvania: Rodale Press Book Division, 1974. p. 430-433.

JARVIS, D.C., M.D. Folk Medicine...A Vermont Doctor's Guide to Good Health. New York: Holt, Rinehart and Winston, 1958.

JARVIS, D.C., M.D. Vermont Folk Medicine and Arthritis (Excerpt from D.C. Jarvis, M.D. Arthritis and Folk Medicine. New York: Holt, Rinehart and Winston, 1960.)

JENKINS, D.J.A., A.R. Leeds, C. Newton, and J.H. Cummings. Lancet 1, 1975. pp. 1116-1117.

JONES, J. The High Calcium Diet. Chicago: Nightingale-Conant Corporation, 1986.

KALLAN, Carla. Prevention Oct. 1991: 39-43

KARAPINAR, M. and S.A. Gonul. International Journal of Food Microbiology Aug 1992: 343-7.

KARAPINAR, M. and S.A. Gonul. International Journal of Food Microbiology Jul 1992: 261-4.

KAUFMAN, M.B. Pediatric Emergency Care Feb 1992: 27-8.

KIRK, Ronald S., ed. Pearson's Composition and Analysis of Foods. New York: Wiley, 1991. pp. 458-468.

KORN, Carl, M.D., Assistant Clinical Professor of Dermatology, University of Southern California in Tkac, Debora, et al. The Doctor's Book of Home Remedies. New York: Bantam Books, 1991. p. 629.

KRATZER, Brice L., and Dallas W. Sandt. Nutrition: Where Have All These Labels Been? Nutrition Awareness System. 100-103.

LALANNE, Elaine with Richard Benyo. Total Juicing. Plume, Penguin Group, 1992. pp. 58-59.

LARSON, David. Mayo Clinic Family Health Book. William Morrow and Company, Inc., 1990. pp. 676-677.

LEE, Sally. New Theories on Diet and Nutrition. p. 45.

LEGRO, William, ed. High-Speed Healing...The Fastest, Safest and Most Effective Shortcuts to Lasting Relief. Pennsylvania: Rodale Press, 1991. pp. 57, 275.

LEVEILLE, G.A. and H.E. Sauberlich Journal of Nutrition 88, 1966: 209-217.

LEVIN, B. and D. Horwitz. Medical Clinics of North America 63(5), 1979. pp. 1043-1055.

LI, Jun Yao, Phillip R. Taylor, Bing Li, Sanford Dawsey, Guo-Qing Wang, Abby G. Ershow, Wande Gua, Shu-Fan Liu, Chung S. Yang, Qiong Shen, Wen Wang, Steven D. Mark, Xiao-Nong Zou, Peter Greenwald, Yang-Ping Wu, William J. Blot. Journal of National Cancer Institute 15 Sept 1993: 1492-1498.

LIN, T.M., K.S. Kim, E. Karvinen, and A.C. Ivy. American Journal of Physiology 188 (1), 1957: 66-70.

MARTIN, J.C. and I. Audley. Medical Journal of Australia 6 Aug 1990: 164-6.

MENTER, Marcia. Redbook Jan 1993: 30-32

MINDELL, Earl, R.Ph., Ph.D. Earl Mindell's Herb Bible. New York: Fireside a division of Simon & Schuster, 1992. pp. 42, 79-80.

MODAN, Barich. Lancet 18 July 1992: 162(3).

MORGAN, Brian L.G., Dr. Nutrition Prescription-Strategies for Preventing and Treating 50 Common Diseases. New York: Crown Publishers, Inc. p. 183, 276-279.

MOWREY, Daniel B., Ph.D. The Scientific Validation of Herbal Medicine. Connecticut: Keats Publishing, Inc. pp. 39-46, 89-96.

NAHATA, M.C., D. Hembekides, and K.I. Koranyi. Chemotherapy vol 32, issue 2: 178-82.

JOURNAL of the National Cancer Institute September 15, 1993. Philip R. Taylor, M.D., Sc.D., Jun-Yao Li, M.D., and Bing Li, M.D.

NOTELOVITS, M., and M. Ware. Stand Tall! Gainesville, FL: Triad Publishing Company, 1982.

"NUTRITION Intervention Trials." Journal of the National Cancer Institute 15 Sept 1993: 1445.

OMEGA Nutrition. "Apple Cider Vinegar." Omega Nutrition: Vancouver, B.C. V5X3Y3.

OTHMER, Kirk. Encyclopedia of Chemical Technology New York: Interscience-a division of Wiley, 1963. pp. 254-265.

PEARSON, Durk and Sandy Shaw. Life Extension...A Practical Scientific Approach-Adding Years to Your Life and Life to Your Years. pp. 296-300.

PEARSON, Durk and Sandy Shaw. The Life Extension Weight Loss Program. New York: Doubleday & Co., Inc., 1986. pp. 29-47.

PENNINGTON, Jean A.T., PH.D., R.D., and Helen Nichols Church, B.S. Bowes and Church's Food Values of Portions Commonly Used. New York: Harper & Row Publishers, 1979.

RADER, Lora. Countryside & Small Stock Journal March-April 1993: 14(1).

REDDY, B.S., K. Watanabe, and A. Sheinfil. Journal of Nutrition 110, 1980. pp. 1247-1254.

RODIN, Judith. American Journal of Clinical Nutrition 1990: 51: 428-35.

ROSANOFF, A., AND D.H. CALLOWAY. New England Journal of Medicine 306:239, 1982.

SCOTT, CYRIL. Complete Cider Vinegar. Wellingborough: Thorsons, 1987.

SOLOMON, Caleb. Wall Street Journal 30 Sept. 1992: A1, A4.

SOUTHGATE, D.A.T. American Journal of Clinical Nutrition 31, 1978.

STRAUCH, G., P. Pandos, and H. Bricaire. Journal of Clinical Endocrinology and Metablolism April 1971: 582(3).

STORY, J.A., D. Kritchevsky, and M.A. Eastwood. Dietary Fibers. Chemistry and Nutrition. New York: Academic Press, 1979. p. 49.

"SWIMMER'S Ear." University of California at Berkeley Wellness Letter Aug 1991: 6.

"SWIMMER'S Ear, Itchy Ears and Ear Fungus." American Academy of Otolaryngology-Head and Neck Surgery 1984.

TKAC, Debora, et al. The Doctors Book of Home Remedies. New York: Bantam Books, 1991.

TRENTHAN, David. Science 24 Sept 1993.

TROWELL, H. American Journal of Clinical Nutrition 31(10), 1978. pp. S3-S11.

UNITED States. Department of Agriculture. Nutritive Value of American Foods-In Common Units. Washington, D.C.: GPO, 1975.

UNITED States. Department of Health and Human Sciences. The Surgeon General's Report on Nutrition and Health. Warner Books, 1989.

UNITED States. Department of Health and Human Sciences. The Surgeon General's Report on Nutrition and Health. DHHS (PHS) Publication No. 88-50210. Washington, D.C.: U.S. Government Printing Office. GPO Stock No. 017-001-00465-1.

"VARIETIES of Vinegars Add Taste for Calorie Counters. " The Washington Post.

VISSER, Margaret. Saturday Night June 1992: 42.

WALSH, B.A. Journal of ET Nursing Jul-Aug 1992: 110-3.

"WATER in the Ear." University of California, Berkeley Wellness Letter. August 1987

WILEN, Joan and Lydia Wilen. Chicken Soup and Other Folk Remedies. New York: Fawcett Columbine, 1984. p. 26.

WISE Encyclopedia of Cookery, The. New York: Wm. H. Wise & Co., Inc., 1949. p. 1219.

"WINNING the Fiber Game." University of California, Berkeley Wellness Letter. March 1990: 3.

WOLMAN, Patricia Giblin, Ed.D., R.D. Journal of the American Dietetic Association Sept 1987: 1211-1214.

No one book could ever contain all the useful remedies, cleaning shortcuts, and secrets of the good people I've met through my travels. Most likely you, too, know about healing remedies that have been passed down from generation to generation.

And so, I would love to hear from you. If you have a remedy, or other useful advice, you would like to share with others, please use this page (or a sheet of plain paper) to share it with me.* If I am able to use it in an upcoming edition of a remedies book, I will send you a free copy of the new book.

Thank you, and my best wishes for a long and healthy life,

Emily Thacker

_____

_____

_____

_____

_____

Please indicate (yes or no) whether I may use your name if I use this helpful advice:

❏ YES, please credit this remedy to _____
(Please Print)

❏ NO, please use my remedy, but do not use my name in the book.
(Either way, Yes or No, if I use your remedy, I'll send you a free copy of the new edition of home remedies!)

Your remedy can be one which uses Vinegar or simply one that you feel others would like to know about.

My favorite chapter in "The Vinegar Book" is:

_____

_____

The helpful remedy I most appreciated in "The Vinegar Book" appears on page _____ ,
and tells how to: _____

_____

_____

What I liked best about "The Vinegar Book" was:

_____

_____

_____

_____

If you have any comments or experiences to add to the information you've read in
this collection, or if you have information for subsequent editions, please address your
letters to:

> Emily Thacker
> 718 - 12th Street N.W., Box 24500
> Canton, Ohio 44701

- -

Use this coupon to order "The Vinegar Book" for a friend or family member -- or copy
the ordering information onto a plain piece of paper and mail to:

> The Vinegar Book
> Dept. F869
> 718 - 12th Street N.W.
> Box 24500
> Canton, Ohio 44701

Preferred Customer Reorder Form

Order this...	If you want a book on...	Cost...	Number of Copies...
Mind Power Memory Magic	New scientific breakthroughs promise Super Memory, yours at any age—Plus FREE bonus: Secrets of Pep, Vim and Vigor...	$9.95	
Home Remedies from the Old South	Hundreds of little known old-time remedies for aches & pains, cleaning & beauty.	$9.95	
The Garlic Book	Scientific discoveries backup old-time claims for garlic's ability to heal. Emily Thacker brings you a mix of old remedies, medical facts and healthy recipes.	$9.95	
Emily's Book of Health Without Drugs	Emily Thacker presents the best of alternative medicine, along with newest scientific breakthroughs. Secret healing ways from the Far East, new vinegar uses & old-time remedies.	$9.95	
How To Use Trusts To Protect You From Catastrophic Loss	How to use Living Trusts to protect your cash, home and valuables from nursing home and other catastrophic costs.	$9.95	
The Honey Book	Honey's magical mix of carbohydrates and minerals. Honey has a healthy dose of the B complex vitamins in its luscious golden liquid. And there are hundreds of cooking hints.	$9.95	
The Vinegar Book	Apple Cider Vinegar's magical mix of tart good taste and germ killing acid. Vinegar has more than 30 important nutrients, a dozen minerals, plus vitamins, amino acids, enzymes — even pectin for a healthy heart. And, there are hundreds of cooking hints.	$9.95	

Any combination of the above $9.95 items qualifies for the following discounts...

Order any 2 items for:
$15.95

Order any 3 items for:
$19.95

Order any 4 items for:
$24.95

Order any 5 items for
$29.95

Order any 6 items for:
$34.95
and receive 7th item FREE

Total NUMBER of $9.95 items		
Total COST of $9.95 items		
Emily Thacker's Collected Works — Limited collector edition of over 1,200 of Emily Thacker's best natural health folk remedies in a gigantic 8 1/2 x 11-inch volume. Four complete books cover home remedies for Vinegar, Garlic, Old South Home Remedies and alternative Health Without Drugs methods.	*$24.95* ~~$29.95~~	
Postage & Handling		$2.95
TOTAL		

90-DAY MONEY-BACK GUARANTEE

Please rush me the items marked above. I understand that I must be completely satisfied or I can return any item within 90 days with proof of purchase for a full and prompt refund of my purchase price.

I am enclosing $_____ by: ❏ Check ❏ Money Order (Make checks payable to Tresco)

Charge my: ❏ VISA ❏ MasterCard Card No. _____

Signature _____ Exp. Date _____

Name _____

Address _____

City _____ State _____ Zip _____

Telephone Number (_____) _____

For Faster Service
Credit Card customers call
TOLL FREE 1-800-772-7285
Operator Q586

Mail To: **TRESCO PUBLISHERS** • 718 - 12th St. N.W., Box 24500, Dept. Q586 • Canton, Ohio 44701
Customer Service (216) 453-8311

MEMORY MAGIC

Is your memory as good as it once was? See how to remember more things longer, learn facts faster, make fewer mistakes and release the full power of your mind.

You need never lose your keys, forget where you parked your car or miss an important meeting. If forgetfulness has made your life miserable - you NEED Memory Magic.

FREE BONUS: SECRETS OF PEP, VIM AND VIGOR...

HOME REMEDIES FROM THE OLD SOUTH

Emily Thacker's original collection of old-time remedies. Hundreds of little-known cures from yesteryear on how to lose weight, beautify skin, help arthritis. A collection of more than 700 remedies Grandma used for colds, sinus, sexual dysfunction, gout, hangovers, asthma, urinary infections, headaches, and appetite control. Over 150 beauty secrets using staples in your fridge such as lemons, cream, tomatoes, flowers, eggs, honey and vinegar.

FREE BONUS: THE INCREDIBLE MAGIC OF HONEY & VINEGAR FOR HEALING, HEALTH & WEIGHT LOSS shows you how these two vitamin and mineral packed health foods have been used for better health, younger-looking skin, and safer cleaning.

NEW
THE GARLIC BOOK

Hundreds of little known old-time cures using garlic's almost magical ability to heal and protect. Medical science has lots to say about this wonderful little bulb, some of which may surprise you! Ways to use garlic inside and outside of the body, what's the best kind, and how to cultivate your own year round supply. FREE BONUS: NATURAL WAYS TO BETTER HEALTH.

NEW
EMILY'S BOOK OF HEALTH WITHOUT DRUGS

Emily Thacker's look at today's health choices, combined with chapters by health care professionals. Easy to understand explanations of the newest medical science breakthroughs and the best of the old-time home remedies. This collection of health hints includes: new ways to use vinegar and other old-time health tips, experiences and comments of doctors, public health officials, therapists, and others in the world of conventional and alternative health care. Exciting old and new ways to manage pain and feel better.

HOW TO USE TRUSTS TO PROTECT YOU FROM CATASTROPHIC LOSS

The rich have always been able to use Trusts to protect their estates for heirs. Now there is easy to understand and use information on how people with modest estates can use Living Trusts. And, you'll see how the right kind of Trust can protect you, RIGHT NOW, from the cost of a long nursing home stay. You need this information to make sure you are doing everything possible to guard your life savings from sudden, unexpected loss.

NEW
THE HONEY BOOK

Emily Thacker's newest collection of remedies has hundreds of ways to use honey for health & healing, cooking & preserving. Ancient honey uses, as well as newest scientific facts. See how honey's mix of essential flower oils, proteins, phosphorus, carbohydrates, calcium, niacin, potassium, iron, trace elements and enzymes aid good health.

THE VINEGAR BOOK

Emily Thacker's collection of old-time remedies has hundreds of ways to use vinegar for health & healing, cooking & preserving, cleaning & polishing. Learn Cleopatra's secret way with vinegar, as well as newest uses straight from hospital emergency rooms! See how vinegar's unique mix of more than 30 nutrients, nearly a dozen minerals, plus amino acids, enzymes, and pectin for a healthy heart has been used for thousands of years.

NEW
FOUR EMILY THACKER BOOKS — OVER 1,200 FOLK REMEDIES — NOW IN ONE GIGANTIC COLLECTOR EDITION

Imagine! You can own the Collector Edition of the best-selling Vinegar Book, Home Remedies from the Old South, Emily's Book of Health Without Drugs and The Garlic Book-- all 272 pages in a huge 8 1/2 x 11-inch volume at less than the usual selling price. Give your family and friends the gift of a longer, healthier, happier life for years to come.